PRAISE FOR *AMERICAN WHITELASH*

"*American Whitelash* offers a livid account of the hydra-like capacity of white supremacist ideas not just to survive but to flourish. . . . It's an infuriating, radicalizing read. . . . A good primer on the unhealthy state of the nation as we enter election season."

—*Washington Post Book World*

"Lowery's galvanizing new book charts the cycle of racial progress and white backlash that has repeatedly played out through U.S. history. Beginning with President Barack Obama's 2008 election, Lowery investigates contemporary systems of white supremacy and how they helped bring about the unprecedented political rise of Donald Trump. Combining historical research with critical yet empathetic firsthand reporting, the bestselling author of *They Can't Kill Us All* delivers a searing examination of the movement."

—*Time*

"Reveals the tensions latent in our common conceptions of racism by probing recent surges in white supremacist violence. . . . [Lowery] is a lively narrative reporter with a keen eye for detail, and his prose can be devastatingly vivid."

—*Washington Post*

"Lowery provides urgent, necessary perspective. . . . A masterful blend of narrative history and empathetic reporting."

—*Kirkus Reviews* (starred review)

ALSO BY WESLEY LOWERY

"They Can't Kill Us All":
Ferguson, Baltimore, and a New Era in
America's Racial Justice Movement

AMERICAN WHITELASH

A CHANGING NATION AND THE COST OF PROGRESS

WESLEY LOWERY

MARINER BOOKS   *New York   Boston*

HarperCollins books may be purchased for educational, business,
or sales promotional use. For information, please email the Special
Markets Department at SPsales@harpercollins.com.

A hardcover edition of this book was published in 2023 by
Mariner Books.

FIRST MARINER BOOKS PAPERBACK EDITION PUBLISHED 2024.

Designed by Chloe Foster

Library of Congress Control Number: 2023936538

ISBN 978-0-06-332091-8

24 25 26 27 28 LBC 5 4 3 2 1

For Kevin Gorczyca,

who taught me that the purest and deepest forms of love come not in spite of our differences, but because of them.

And for all who have been victims of the violence and terror of our era.

A storyteller can attempt to tell the human tale, can make a galaxy out of the chaos, can point to the fact that some people survived even as most people died. And can remind us that the swallows still sing around the smokestacks.

—JANE YOLEN, *The Devil's Arithmetic*, 1988

CONTENTS

A Note on Language   xiii

PART I: White Grievance   1

PART II: In Defense of American Whiteness   29

PART III: White Radicalization   89

PART IV: An American Nazi's Final Bark   137

PART V: A Movement Rises   167

Epilogue   225

Acknowledgments   239

Notes   241

A NOTE ON LANGUAGE

In the pages of this book, I use the lowercase for *black* and *white* when used to describe racial groups. It is currently popular to capitalize the *b* in *black*, in acknowledgment of and in reverence for the history, experience, and culture of black Americans. But at this moment in our history—amid pervasive racial violence and destructive white grievance—I fear capitalization provides fodder for those who preach race as a biological reality, as opposed to a societal construction. While racism is deadly real, race itself is a fiction.

PART I

WHITE GRIEVANCE

There is no Negro problem in America.

The problem of race in America, insofar as that problem is related to packets of melanin in men's skins, is a white problem. And in order to solve that problem we must seek its source, not in the Negro but in the white American (in the process by which he was educated, in the needs and complexes he expresses through racism) and in the structure of the white community (in the power arrangements and the illicit uses of racism in the scramble for scarce values: power, prestige, income).

The depth and intensity of the race problem in America is, in part, a result of a 100-year flight from that unpalatable truth.

—LERONE BENNETT JR., *Ebony* MAGAZINE, AUGUST 1965

1

IT FEELS SOMEWHAT SILLY NOW, more than a decade later, to dwell on the images, feelings, and sounds of that November night. To recall the gravity of the moment, and the jubilation. Because to revisit the evening of Barack Obama's election is to venture into a world that feels foreign now. November 4, 2008, was a collective moment of true, unabashed hope.

"If there is anyone out there who still doubts that America is a place where all things are possible, who still wonders if the dream of our founders is alive in our time, who still questions the power of our democracy, tonight is your answer," declared Obama, then a forty-seven-year-old junior senator from Illinois, who moments earlier had become the first person of African descent to be elected president of the United States.

His words rang thunderously through the crowd of thousands who had assembled at Chicago's Grant Park—named after the former president and Union general who vanquished the Confederacy and its villainous effort to preserve slavery and who, unlike many others of his time, supported black enfranchisement. For hours, the forceful chants of Obama's campaign slogan—"Yes we can!"—had echoed through the crisp autumn air. But now, as Obama spoke, the crowd fell into a solemn silence.

Almost all the footage from that night cuts at some point to a tearful Jesse Jackson, the Chicago reverend and civil rights activist whose years of labor to register southern black voters, rewrite Democratic Party rules, and forge a multiracial coalition as part of his own campaigns for the presidency had laid the pathway across which Obama's campaign would dash to a decisive victory over Republican John McCain. Also present at Grant Park was Oprah Winfrey, the trailblazing African American broadcaster turned media mogul, and one of Obama's earliest political boosters. "It feels like America did the right thing," she remarked in an interview with a CNN reporter. "It feels like there's a shift in consciousness."

Change, the president-elect insisted, had come—a promise that left his lips 389 years after the first Africans had arrived, in chains, in the land that would become the British colonies; 151 years after the nation's highest court ruled that Dred Scott, an enslaved man attempting to sue for his freedom, had no standing to bring a suit because in the eyes of the law he was property and not a person; and 143 years since the conclusion of the Civil War that had cleaved the country in two and left more than a half million dead.

Obama launched his audacious campaign for the White House—in the name of "common hopes and common dreams"—in February 2007, in Springfield, Illinois, a site dripping with history. Springfield was Abraham Lincoln's hometown. And it was where, a century earlier, a white mob had burned black homes and businesses, leaving seven people dead and hundreds injured; violence that, in turn, helped spark the founding of the National Association for the Advancement of Colored People (NAACP), a leading voice in opposition to the racial terrorism of Jim Crow–era lynchings and in advocacy for full black citizenship and suffrage.

Now, twenty-one months later, Obama assured a nation crafted from the clay of inequity that it had finally eradicated the injustice upon which it had laid its foundation. A country built on the subjugation of black people had now voted to place a black man in its highest office. As author and journalist Ta-Nehisi Coates would later write: "Obama appealed to a belief in innocence—in particular white innocence—that ascribed the country's historical errors more to misunderstanding . . . than to any deliberate malevolence or widespread racism. This appeal attracted people because it allowed them to feel that America was good."

On MSNBC, legendary anchorman Tom Brokaw deemed Obama's election a "profoundly important passage out of the deep shadows of our racist past that began with that first slave offloaded on a ship." The momentousness resonated around the world. Cable news split screens showed jubilant crowds filling the streets of the small Kenyan farming village where Obama's father had been born. OBAMA: RACIAL BARRIER FALLS IN DECISIVE VICTORY, the *New York Times* would declare on its front page the following morning.

So, what the hell happened? Because it's clear, with the benefit of even a decade of historical hindsight, that the election of a black president did not usher us from the shadows of our racist past; rather it led us down a perilous path and into a decade and a half (and counting) of explicit racial thrashing.

The years that followed Obama's election would see two long-simmering racial movements burst to the fore of mainstream politics.

The first of these was a nativist movement of white Americans that questioned the validity of the president's citizenship, his Christian faith, and his fidelity to America itself. For his eight years in office, Obama would have no more consistent and persistent foe. This opposition was fanned by leaders on the political Right— many of them media figures, some of them elected officials—who preached a politics of racial agitation: fear of immigrants and Muslims, contempt for black public figures and elected officials, and rebellion against government attempts to address racial inequalities. This movement wielded inflammatory rhetoric to appeal to the real fear held by many Americans, of varying political affiliations, that the country had irreversibly changed in ways that left them unheard and underserved, exposed and vulnerable.

The Obama years were an era in which the murderous brutality of the Islamic terrorist network ISIS had renewed for many their post-9/11 concerns about Muslim terrorism. New census forecasts had many Americans imagining fundamental demographic changes to the face and feel of their nation. The passage of the Affordable Care Act represented a crushing blow to the small-government conservatives who, since Democratic president Franklin D. Roosevelt instituted the New Deal in the 1930s to dig the United States out of the Great Depression, had argued that the expansion of federal government services represented a march toward socialist doom. President George W. Bush's tax cuts and the Obama bank bailouts had left many working-class Americans across the political spectrum convinced that the system was rigged against them and that they had been left behind. Decades of activism resulted in major legal victories for LGBTQ Americans, including the U.S. Supreme Court's legalizing same-sex marriage, that left social and religious conservatives convinced that they had lost what for years had been among the most frantically simmering culture wars. And violence and economic calamity in Central and South America sent waves of migrants to the southern U.S. border, underscoring a decades-long failure in Washington to come up with and enforce a coherent immigration policy.

All of this occurred alongside the ongoing racial integration of both public and private life—due in part to affirmative action and diversity and inclusion policies seeking to rectify the historic exclusion of racial minorities from such spaces—forcing a critical mass of white Americans to increasingly share space with their black and brown neighbors, or to at least imagine that they would have to someday soon. Even pop culture provided them little escape: A new set of spinoffs of the *Rocky* movie franchise, the ultimate white ethnic American underdog story, featured a black protagonist; *Spider-Man*'s Peter Parker was recast as Miles Morales, an Afro Latino teen; and *Black Panther*, with a mostly black ensemble, became the most significant superhero story of the era. Even as they occupied a nation structured, from its inception, to advantage people who looked like them, the post-Obama era saw white Americans become convinced, in the aggregate, that they were the targets of antiwhite bigotry and being systematically discriminated against.

In 2011, researchers from Tufts and Harvard Universities interviewed black and white Americans about how they believed issues of race in the United States had changed since the 1950s, when the civil rights movement began to reorder American society and secure full citizenship rights for black Americans. Both study groups agreed that racism against black people had decreased, but white people believed that it had declined faster and more significantly than black respondents did. The white people acknowledged antiblack bias in America, but said they believed the country was also afflicted with antiwhite bias and that *it* was the more prevalent form of racial prejudice.

Two corresponding polls in 1986 and 2015 documented a surge of American pessimism that was particularly stark among white respondents: in 1986, 10 percent of white respondents between the ages of eighteen and thirty-five said that "the American dream" is "not really alive." By 2015, that number had tripled to 29 percent. Among white respondents who said that "the American dream"—however they personally defined it—meant something to them, a majority said they believed it had become harder to achieve.

By the end of the Obama presidency one year later, another poll found that 55 percent of white Americans believed the country discriminated against them racially.

The Obama years also prompted deep dissension within his own political base, driven by movements of progressives, young voters, and black and brown people.

While much of the activist energy on the Left during the Bush-43 years had been concentrated in the antiwar movement, though certainly not exclusively, the protest chants of the Obama years would concentrate largely on a slate of perceived domestic failings. The Occupy Wall Street demonstrations captured working-class frustrations with income inequality and the excesses of capitalism. A rising generation of immigration activists demanded that Obama halt deportations and create a legal pathway to citizenship for at least some of the millions of undocumented migrants living in the United States.

Frustrations with the limitations of a black president prompted a new era in the American civil rights movement, one that rose as a direct response to the perceived limitations of the "black faces in high places" politics that had taken hold in the decades since the civil rights movement. This movement, known colloquially as "Black Lives Matter," argued for structural and systemic changes to create a country in which the outstanding invoice from centuries of explicit inequity would finally be paid through aggressive measures to rid our society of the discrimination baked into our systems and institutions, as well as government intervention to remedy inequities that persist even after equality under the law has been established and literal reparations granted to communities and people systematically harmed.

For black Americans who had spent decades working within the system, the election of a black president had allowed them to dream even bigger. And for the young black men and women who had turned out in droves to cast their first-ever votes for Barack Obama, the backlash to his presidency and the constraints on his rule only heightened the urgency.

Republicans had mobilized in response to Obama's election, vowing to make him a "one-term president" and working across the country to implement the most sweeping set of voting restrictions the nation had seen since the Jim Crow era. Just one year into the forty-fourth president's first term brought the rise of the Tea Party movement, a right-wing rebellion as much against Republican elites as the Democratic administration that, as had been true of past populist efforts on the Right, contained elements of racial bigotry that were in many cases thinly veiled and in others completely unmasked and explicit. While the movement was concerned most vocally with the nation's economic health and the perception that average Americans had been left behind, studies and polling have consistently shown that it was made up of white voters more likely to hold racially prejudiced views than the white population at large and who adopted among their chief slogans the need to "take our country back."

The killings of Trayvon Martin (by a neighborhood watchman) and Oscar Grant, Eric Garner, Michael Brown, and Tamir Rice (by police officers) sent scores of black demonstrators into the streets to demand accountability and a reconsideration of the institution of American policing. For much of Obama's second term, the postings of viral videos showing the killings of black men and women at the hands of police seemed a near-daily occurrence, followed, many times, by mass protests and, in some cases, violent urban uprisings and riots.

The achievement of what had been until very recently an unimaginable political accomplishment—the election of a black president—had provided permission for black Americans to demand even bigger victories. In 2014 Coates published one of the era's seminal pieces of journalism in *The Atlantic*, "The Case for Reparations," bringing an argument present for generations among black activists and organizers into the political mainstream. Five years later, *The New York Times Magazine* would publish "The 1619 Project," the brainchild of Nikole Hannah-Jones. The initiative argued that our very historical conception of our nation begin not with the revolution that freed the early Americans from British colonial rule but instead with the arrival of the first ships carrying a cargo of enslaved Africans more than a century earlier.

Meanwhile, each new death, each trending hashtag, each new episode exemplifying racial inequity and injustice—a water crisis in the predominantly black city of Flint, Michigan; a young white supremacist gunning down nine black worshipers in a South Carolina church; the backlash to NFL quarterback Colin Kaepernick and other professional football players protesting police violence by silently taking a knee during the pre-kickoff singing of the national anthem—provided a fresh reminder not of the black presidency's promise but of its limitations.

"I was 17 when President-elect Obama walked across the stage in Grant Park with his Black, beautiful, accomplished wife and their two young Black daughters to give his acceptance speech," the poet and essayist Camonghne Felix wrote in early 2022. "I'm 30 now and staring down the greatest threat to African American voting rights in generations. A climate crisis threatens the livelihoods of the Black and poor, of the Black and coastal, of the Black and immigrant. We face a wealth gap that has only worsened in the last decade, leaving Black communities even more vulnerable to the failures of late-stage capitalism than they already were before the First Black Presidency. . . .

"We had set the bar too high," Felix continued. "We expected our first Black president to decry the actions of the racist police, to call off the dogs and stand unequivocally with protesters—to somehow inherit Martin Luther King Jr.'s project of disarming white supremacy and see it through to a different end. He didn't. He hedged and stood tall in two-sides-ism, calling angry civilians thugs and their uprising a counterproductive distraction to the more 'peaceful' protesters doing things 'the right way.' What we expected of the Obama administration was beyond what the framework of the presidency allowed."

• • •

These diametrically opposed movements—one built atop the centurylong battle for black humanity; the other a repository of white racial grievance—fed off each other, each driving citizens into the arms of the other. As a young, black protest movement pushed the political establishment to consider more drastic action on racial inequity, the white backlash to a black presidency and the changing nation grew in size, strength, and intensity.

After two terms, Obama was replaced by Donald Trump, a reality television star who had installed himself as the leader of the growing movement of white backlash. Trump harnessed the frustration of those who believed they had been left behind by Washington elites numb to their economic and cultural needs and who believed they occupied an America forever changed from the one that older white Americans remembered wistfully (if not always accurately) and younger white Americans had once imagined they would grow old in.

Trump explicitly played to the racial discomfort of the Republican Party's nearly all-white political base and expanded it to include pockets of working-class white ethnic voters who had previously supported Democrats.

His first forays into politics in the early 2010s included vocal opposition to the so-called Ground Zero mosque, an attempt to turn a building two blocks away from the World Trade Center into an Islamic cultural center, and vows to "investigate" Obama's citizenship based on the racist (and patently untrue) "birther" conspiracy theory that speculated that the forty-fourth president had been born abroad and was thus ineligible for the presidency. As a presidential candidate in 2016, Trump's central pledge was to "build the wall" on the southern border in order to keep out Hispanic immigrants.

While Obama had embraced the growing black protest movement—convening a policing task force to facilitate reform in departments across the country and inviting young black protest leaders to the White House for what ended up being the longest meeting of his presidency—Trump cast it as his foil. He railed against the protesters who had taken to the streets, sought out a lengthy string of police union endorsements, and leaned into the rhetoric of law and order while playing up the images of urban unrest—the same type of unrest that had, just a few generations earlier, contributed to the white flight from the cities and into the suburbs.

"Trump put an unapologetic voice to white fear," journalist Roland Martin and Leah Lakins write in their book *White Fear: How the Browning of America Is Making White Folks Lose Their Minds*, defining white fear as "the unwillingness to share power and resources and allow for the redefinition of America's morals, values, and principles."

Trump received nearly sixty-three million votes in 2016, cast overwhelmingly by white Americans, including millions of Obama-to-Trump voters, most of them white. "Racial conservatives and those with the most punitive immigration views are moving right and were the most likely to switch to Trump in 2016," concluded the authors of a study of such voters published in the journal *Public Opinion Quarterly*.

There is no question that a number of factors contributed to the Trump victory, in addition to the racial dynamics: the decades-long demonization of his Democratic opponent, Hillary Clinton; misogyny toward her historic candidacy; tactical errors committed by her campaign; and an electorate sincerely opposed to her proposals and policies. What's more, the former secretary of state and first lady was victimized by coordinated Russian interference in our election and the FBI's response. Intense partisanship, particularly around the issues of abortion and immigration, and the earnestly held economic fears of many voters and growing distrust of elite institutions that had infected the bloodstreams of both parties also factored into her losing the electoral college despite finishing with almost three million more votes than Trump.

The result of it all, though, was that after the eight years in which America had its first black president, a coalition of aggrieved white Americans elevated a white racial demagogue to the Oval Office.

Speaking on CNN on the night of Trump's election, activist Van Jones declared, "We've talked about everything but race tonight. We've talked about income, we've talked about class. We've talked about region. This was a whitelash. It was a whitelash against a changing country. It was a whitelash against a black president."

Once inaugurated, one of Trump's first acts was to ban much of the Muslim world from entering the country. Under his administration, historic steps that had been taken under Obama to curb police abuses in black communities were abandoned, and thousands of migrant children were forcibly separated from their families at the southern border. Within a year of Trump's election, armed throngs of neo-Nazis marched through the streets of Charlottesville, Virginia, chanting, "The Jews will not replace us!" Black Americans, Muslims, and immigrants feared they would fall victim to violent assaults committed by perpetrators who had arguably been incited by the president's language. Often they did.

When a once-in-a-lifetime virus began ravaging the globe in early 2020, President Trump suggested it would magically disappear. It did not. Instead, Covid-19 drowned black, Latino, and indigenous communities with a special devastation that revealed anew the extent to which Americans may reside in one country but live in very different worlds. When it came time to vote again in November 2020, a bitterly divided nation removed Trump from the Oval Office. But the events of the months that followed further underscored the racial divide planted before our founding, watered throughout centuries of American life and aided still by the stubborn refusal to uproot its rotten tares.

On January 6, 2021, the day after Georgia elected both its first black senator and its first Jewish senator to give Democrats control of the upper congressional chamber, a violent mob—summoned to the National Mall by President Trump, incited that day and for weeks in advance by his lie that the election had been stolen from him—stormed the Capitol building in DC. They were drunk with indignation and fueled by baseless, often-racist conspiracy theories. They threatened the lives of Vice President Mike Pence, Speaker of the House Nancy Pelosi, and the entire legislative branch, as Congress gathered to certify the results of the electoral college. Capitol Police officers were attacked as congressional offices were ransacked by insurrectionists wearing Trump hats and waving Confederate battle flags.

The University of Chicago Project on Security and Threats analyzed 377 of the people who faced criminal charges following January 6 and concluded that many of them lived in communities where the white population had been declining. "The people alleged by authorities to have taken the law into their hands on Jan. 6 typically hail from places where nonwhite populations are growing fastest," wrote CPOST director Robert A. Pape.

The months and years to come would see the growth of the extreme and potent political movement witnessed on January 6, determined to restrict voting access for groups of voters they considered likely Democrats and to punish elected officials who dared to play a role in certifying Donald Trump's 2020 defeat. To date, this conspiratorial movement remains among the most powerful and mobilized forces within American politics.

2

IT IS CLEAR THAT THE election of a black president did not herald a new era of American racial harmony. Yet this is a conclusion that should have never required hindsight. As much should have been clear from the beginning—and was, to those who bothered to look. At the same time that the post-Obama era saw the consolidation of two long-simmering mainstream racial movements, it also prompted the resurgence of a third: the nation's most notorious, violent political ideology.

On the very November night that President-elect Obama addressed the audience of supporters in Grant Park, while much of the nation celebrated joyfully around their living room televisions, a bitter, deadly white supremacist force was being unleashed.

Just hours after Obama's victory had been announced, three white men poured gasoline inside and around the Macedonia Church of God in Christ, a predominantly black congregation in Springfield, Massachusetts, and set it ablaze—ultimately doing $1.6 million in damage. One of the men would later tell police that they were angry that Obama's election meant "blacks and Puerto Ricans would now have more rights than whites."

That same night, a pack of white teenagers drove around Staten Island, New York, with a metal pipe and a stolen police baton, beating up black strangers while chanting "Obama." In Snellville, Georgia, a black family reported that someone had mangled their

Obama lawn signs and left a pizza box full of feces on their lawn. The next morning, on the bus ride to school, their nine-year-old daughter was taunted by a classmate who sneered, "I hope Obama gets assassinated." In New Jersey and Pennsylvania, Democratic voters reported having crosses burned in their yards. Within just one week of Obama's election victory, civil rights groups reported hundreds of incidents of racial violence and vandalism. There would be much more horror to come.

"It was as if my very presence in the White House had triggered a deep-seated panic, a sense that the natural order had been disrupted," Obama himself conceded in the first of his presidential memoirs.

For decades, the hopes of the American white supremacist movement—a collection of avowedly racist individuals and groups who, broadly, believe in biological distinctions between different races and ethnicities and generally advocate racial segregation—had been reliant on this type of violence: individual acts of terror that they hoped would spike racial tensions, lead to both copycat and revenge attacks, and ultimately lead to a race war that would result in the formation of a white-only nation. The beliefs of these self-described racists had, by the time of Obama's election, been pushed out of the political mainstream for roughly a half century, even as the movement itself lay in wait. Now the happenstance of history provided fertile ground for their resurgence.

The year 2008 had been a vital inflection point for white supremacists, featuring two emergency-level developments. The first was an August 2008 report from the U.S. Census Bureau concluding that by 2050, racial minorities would constitute a majority of the American population. Core to the white supremacist ideology had been the belief in systemic "white replacement"—a conspiracy theory that takes several forms but generally argues that through interracial marriage and immigration, the white population is purposefully (by the Jews) being driven to extinction. Now the Census Bureau itself had put out a powerful data point that the white supremacist movement could wield as "proof."

Two months later, the country elected a black man to the Oval Office. David Duke, for decades one of the nation's most prominent white supremacists and founder of the Knights of the Ku Klux Klan, an offshoot of the nation's most notorious terror group, predicted that Obama's election would bring about a "dramatic increase" in the movement's membership, and at least two prominent white supremacist organizations—Stormfront and the Council of Conservative Citizens—saw their websites crash due to the flood of online traffic that came their way following Obama's victory.

As jarring as these developments were for much of the white supremacist movement, they knew, as Duke speculated, that it could all play into their hands. Its adherents have long believed that the majority of white America is too complacent and too manipulated by the media to realize that their race is under a fundamental threat. But in the decade following Obama's election, the mainstream political discourse featured a number of talking points—often delivered unchallenged, in unnuanced ways, by inflammatory messengers—that could have been written by the white supremacists themselves. The white populist forces within the mainstream political Right are distinct, and less nefarious than the long-standing white supremacist movement, yet the former often, knowingly or not, provided quarter to the latter—whose racist messages were destined to have greater salience at a moment when the nation's white majority was feeling increasingly anxious.

"For a number of whites, these monumental social and political trends—including an erosion of whites' majority status and the election of America's first black president—have signaled a challenge to the absoluteness of whites' dominance," writes political scientist Ashley E. Jardina in her 2019 book *White Identity Politics*, which examines data from the American National Election Studies and concludes that white Americans are increasingly viewing the world through the lens of racial identity. "These threats, both real and perceived, have . . . brought to the fore, for many whites, a sense of commonality, attachment, and solidarity with their racial group. They have led a sizeable proportion of whites to believe that their racial group, and the benefits that group enjoys, are endangered. As a result, this racial solidarity now plays a central role in the way many whites orient themselves to the political and social world."

Efforts to paint Obama as a foreign, Muslim invader who despised "American exceptionalism" and who, according to then–Fox News host Glenn Beck, held a "deep-seated hatred for white people or the white culture" were precisely the type of political invective that white supremacists were eager to amplify on their message boards. Mainstream histrionics about dirty, criminal immigrants pouring across the southern border and hordes of refugees being imported by, among others, Jewish charities provided the perfect gateway drug to replacement theory. A political discourse that results in lots of white people running Internet searches for statistics about crime and immigration will, inevitably, land many of those people on white supremacist hate sites, which deliberately set themselves up as search-engine-friendly repositories of such information. If a majority of white Americans had become convinced—countering empirical evidence—that a nation constructed from its founding to favor people like them was now actively discriminating against them, white supremacists knew, it's reasonable to expect that some of those people would be convinced to go one step further and embrace the white supremacist belief in a nefarious, Jewish-run plot to perpetuate genocide against white people.

Growing up, Derek Black had quite the pedigree in the world of white nationalism: son of a onetime KKK Grand Wizard named

Don Black, who also founded the neo-Nazi online forum Storm-front. And his mother's previous husband had been none other than David Duke.

Derek was being groomed as Don Black's heir in the white nationalist movement. But in 2013, at the age of twenty-four, he began to repudiate the racist ideologies espoused by his father and other hate groups. Three years later, his transformation was complete: Derek quit the movement and began to speak publicly about his conversion to an anti-racism activist.

In a 2020 interview on the National Public Radio program *All Things Considered*, host Michel Martin asked Black to comment on the recent National Republican Convention, where some of the speeches featured talking points that could have easily doubled as white supremacist propaganda.

"I can think of my godfather David Duke winning his campaign for Louisiana Legislature in the late 1980s," Derek commented. "He never talked about racial epithets. He never attacked groups. It was always the language of the real victims are the silent majority."

As an example, Black pointed to a speech by Patricia McCloskey, a white woman from Saint Louis who, along with her husband, Mark, had pulled guns on Black Lives Matter protesters as they marched past their home in 2020. Using carefully coded racist language, McCloskey declared that Democrats wanted to "abolish the suburbs."

Here is how Black characterized her address: "The real victims are people like you and me against the forces of political correctness; against the forces of discrimination. The real discrimination is against people who look like us—and never going so far as to say white people are the victims, because you always have to avoid being called racist.

"I think you see echoes of that in the McCloskeys talking about the Democrats wanting to totally abolish the suburbs," he observed.

"The message is very clear: that there are people who look like them who live in the suburbs, and there are people who look different from them who are marching in these protests, who are, in their telling, threatening them. That is the essential message of white fear and white power that I've just never seen so explicitly coded."

The results of this kind of language—even coded—can have devastating real-world consequences, of course.

When a twenty-one-year-old white supremacist named Dylann Storm Roof massacred nine black parishioners at the historic Mother Emanuel African Methodist Episcopal Church in Charleston, South Carolina, in June 2015, he did so for the explicit purpose of inciting a race war. While researching online the 2012 shooting death of a black teenager named Trayvon Martin, Roof typed the words "black on White crime" into the Google search bar.

"I have never been the same since that day," Roof would write in a missive posted online prior to the attack. "The first website I came to was the Council of Conservative Citizens"—one of the hate sites that had drawn overwhelming online traffic the night of Obama's election. "There were pages upon pages of these brutal black-on-White murders. I was in disbelief. At this moment, I realized that something was very wrong."

By the time he murdered the black worshippers at Mother Emanuel, Roof had become convinced, through further online "research," that white people in America and Europe had been imperiled by racial minorities and migrants; that white people were biologically superior to black people; and that the future of the white race was threatened by race mixing, which he believed was being encouraged by a global Jewish conspiracy. "By no means should we wait any longer to take drastic action," he declared.

It is impossible to quantify the full extent of the violence seen during this era. Federal hate crime data, which showed spikes in racial violence during the Trump years, are notoriously unreliable due in part to inconsistencies in reporting both by victims and local law enforcement agencies. But the data that do exist suggest that we're living through a moment of heightened white racist aggression, in which the nation's violent underbelly finds itself equal parts frightened and emboldened. In 2017 several colleagues and I at the *Washington Post* analyzed decades of domestic terror attacks and identified a clear trend: attacks by right-wing domestic terrorists and white supremacists were on the rise.

Three years later, in September 2020, FBI director Christopher Wray testified to Congress that, in recent years, the most lethal threat to the American people had been posed by domestic terror attacks, the largest portion of which were committed by white supremacists. Among the insurrectionists who stormed the Capitol on January 6, 2021, were avowed racists determined to keep the man who had incited them in office.

It is worth acknowledging that most of the mainstream political and media figures who traffic in the types of talking points welcomed by white supremacists are likely not doing so knowingly, and they have argued that it is important to be able to advocate openly for things like more restrictive immigration policies or strict law-and-order policing without being accused of racism. When pressed, they insist that they personally abhor racism, and, in the wake of white supremacist violence, political figures across the ideological spectrum are quick to condemn these acts of terror.

Yet a central political question during the years that followed the 2008 election was how much the era's racially inflammatory political rhetoric was inciting—or, at the very least, contributing to—those acts of racial violence, as well as how much of this rhetoric should be permitted in the public square, and how directly responsible are politicians and political figures who traffic in such invective when, inevitably, their talking points are cited as inspiration for a massacre.

In the years after Obama's election, Americans of all stripes watched as racist political rhetoric demonizing black Americans, immigrants, and Jewish people gave way to murder in Charleston, in El Paso, in Charlottesville, in Pittsburgh, and in Buffalo. In all cases, the perpetrators quoted the same words and talking points about diversity, immigration, and the changing complexion of the nation. Mosques were bombed, black pedestrians attacked, synagogues shot up, and immigrants harassed. Neo-Nazis took to the streets, as white supremacist leaders boasted that their movement had been invigorated.

3

AS I BEGAN REPORTING ON the violence that followed the Obama election, I soon realized that it was easier to make sense of what happened by considering this era not as the launch of something new but rather as the continuation of something long in motion.

America's racial history breaks less cleanly into a series of distinct, succeeding time periods than it does into a singular, never-ending tug-of-war between diametrically opposed forces. The story begins with a society structured atop a strict racial caste system, in which both the indigenous populations and the enslaved black people who'd been imported to our shores were considered legally and societally subhuman. Such inherent inequality created the moral imperative that the system be upended: a call answered throughout our history by anti-racist activism, from the slave revolts, to the abolitionists, to the anti-lynching crusaders, to the suffragists, to the civil rights leaders of the midtwentieth century, and to the Black Lives Matter demonstrators in our streets today. Each step toward a more racially just society, each step toward triumph gained by the anti-racist side of the struggle, each periodic collection against the unfulfilled pledges of the American promissory note, in turn, sparks a backlash—a pullback on the rope—from the unjust system's beneficiaries and boosters.

That said, on at least two occasions in our history, this battle prompted fundamental paradigm shifts, upending the very field upon which the battle is fought. The first of these was the Civil War, the end of chattel slavery, and the period of Reconstruction that followed, which resulted in black Americans at last being recognized as fully human, if still not fully equal under the law. The second was the civil rights movement of the 1950s and 1960s, often referred to as a Second Reconstruction in which black Americans won another major change to the foundation of American society, now recognized not just as human but as citizens entitled to equal rights and protections under the law. There has been a tendency, by some historians and scholars, to label our current time as a Third Reconstruction, although that may prove premature. Instead, what we are living through may be a prolonged period of white supremacist backlash.

Both prior periods of Reconstruction were accompanied by a vicious white backlash known as white supremacist Redemption. As historian Peniel Joseph writes: "Redemptionists sought to reinscribe slavery's power relations between Blacks and whites through racial terror, through Black Codes that disenfranchised Black voters, and by ending federal protection for Black citizenship."

"The trigger for white rage, inevitably, is black advancement," writes historian Carol Anderson in *White Rage: The Unspoken Truth of Our Racial Divide*, in which she chronicles the rejection by a significant portion of the white populace of the civil rights advancements and victories of the Second Reconstruction. "White rage doesn't have to wear sheets, burn crosses, or take to the streets. . . . It can look like white flight and private schools and city ordinances and neighborhood watches."

In addition, the decades following the civil rights movement marked a fundamental shift in the white supremacist movement.

For most of American history, white supremacy has been a dispositionally conservative ideology aiming to preserve a racial caste system in which white Americans were the only true citizens. Yet the advent of multiracial democracy through the Second Reconstruction and the perceived browning of America through immigration has forced today's white supremacists to accept as a premise that they're "losing." No longer can they claim, as their forebears did, that they aim to return to the norm of a white supremacist status quo. Today's white supremacist movement is revolutionary—its explicit aim being to overthrow our maturing multiracial democracy.

As election night 2016 gave way to the Trump administration, I kept returning to that idea: the concept of a whitelash.

I was less interested in the debate over how much of Trump's support could be attributed to racial animus than I was captivated by the compounding evidence that his election had emboldened and empowered the most racist among us—people who literally wear sheets and burn crosses. As our politicians and pundits debated what Trump's election said about us as a people, about our enlightenment and racial progress, a dark force was being unleashed across our nation. Avowed white supremacists had taken to the streets.

In May 2017, as protests broke out across the country against the new president, a self-described white nationalist named Jeremy Christian began shouting racist and Islamophobic slurs at two black teenage girls as they rode a light rail train in Portland, Oregon. One of them, a Somali immigrant, was wearing a hijab. When a trio of good Samaritans intervened on their behalf, Christian stabbed all three, killing two of the men.

"Think I stab motherfuckers in the neck for fun? Oh yeah, you're right, I do. I'm a patriot," a handcuffed Christian ranted in the back seat of a police cruiser after he was apprehended. He was later convicted and sentenced to life in prison.

"That's what liberalism gets you," he continued. "I hope they all die. I'm going to say that on the stand. I'm a patriot, and I hope everyone I stabbed died."

Violent acts like these, in this new era of white racial violence, were what made me begin to really reckon with the idea of a whitelash.

I'd spent much of the prior decade as a reporter covering the rise of the Black Lives Matter movement that had been sparked during the Obama years. Now, it seemed, the most urgent story of our time were the other movements that had been prompted by the election of a black president.

For journalists, the hours, and then days, after violent incidents of whitelash bring an uncomfortable routine. We alert the public first to the tragedy. We identify and memorialize the victims. We highlight tales of heroism and heartbreak. And then we set out to answer why.

What compels a white teen to walk into a historic black church and gun down worshippers whose heads are bowed in prayer? What drives a white supremacist to attack a Muslim woman commuting home on a city bus? What prompts a gunman to drive miles from his home to open fire on Hispanic migrants?

There is an obvious futility to the search—there is no satisfying explanation for evil. Yet in moments of chaos and tragedy, human nature demands that we seek answers. For a journalist, the busywork of reporting can be soothing, even if it often feels like we're groping aimlessly in the dark. Understanding the present cannot always be achieved by examining what lays in front of us. Often the answers lie as much in our past as they do in our present, requiring us to turn around and look back.

As I wrote and reported throughout the Trump years, my attention kept turning to these acts of white racial violence. And as I considered my role in this moment—what artifacts of this era I'd create with my pen—I kept returning to the stories of those who fell victim to the hatred that our politics had untethered.

The pages that follow are an exploration of the horror that our era has wrought and an attempt to place a decade of American carnage into the context of American history; a mixture of reporting and observation that leans heavily on the expertise of others and a rich body of historical, journalistic, and sociological work already in existence on these topics. My goal is to be neither comprehensive nor encyclopedic. This book is an attempt to put human faces on the relentless cycle of violence that has defined American history—to put flesh and bone on our discussion of white supremacist terror.

I delve into cases of white racial violence that occurred in the decade following Barack Obama's election. Four took place during the Obama presidency: the murder of Marcelo Lucero on Long Island; a mass shooting at a Sikh temple in Oak Creek, Wisconsin; an anti-Semitic attack in Overland Park, Kansas; and a white supremacist attack on Black Lives Matter protesters in Minneapolis. Two more incidents—the racist rally in Charlottesville, Virginia, and the murder of Richard Collins III in Maryland—happened during the first half of the Trump presidency. All these events force us to grapple with the overlapping bigotries of white supremacy, beyond a black-white lens.

To be clear, in writing about white supremacists, I'm not seeking to analyze or characterize the actions of those who—through their political or policy preferences—can be said to advance a system of white supremacy, intentionally or otherwise. My aim is to examine and explain the proud, avowed white supremacists we see in our streets—defined as those who believe in the genetic and societal superiority of the "white race." Throughout these pages I've also sought to uplift the stories of the real people victimized by their violence, and to chronicle the next churn in the cycle—the new wave of anti-racist activism that has emerged in response to the violence.

The story begins in Patchogue, a small village on Long Island where the coals of whitelash had been simmering for years prior to election night 2008. The election of a black president had sparked great hope. It simultaneously awakened a deep, sick darkness. And just days after Barack Obama's 2008 presidential victory, that darkness came for Marcelo Lucero.

PART II

IN DEFENSE OF AMERICAN WHITENESS

I knew then I had to have a house. A real house. One I could point to. But this isn't it. The house on Mango Street isn't it.
. . .
"No, this isn't my house," I say and shake my head as if shaking could undo the year I've lived here. I don't belong. I don't ever want to come from here.

—ESPERANZA CORDERO, IN SANDRA CISNEROS,
The House on Mango Street

4

THOUGH HIS ENGLISH WAS PASSABLE in public, Joselo Lucero would retreat to the comfort of his native tongue when he could. And so, on nights such as November 4, 2008, he'd plop down next to his roommate, sink into the couch in the living room of their second-floor walk-up, and turn on a TV that was already tuned to Univision.

It had been a decade and a half since Joselo had followed his older brother from Gualaceo, the farming village in Ecuador where they'd been raised, to Patchogue, a small blue-collar community on the South Shore of Long Island. In all that time, he couldn't recall another moment of such frantic anticipation. That evening, Joselo watched and listened as the sights and sounds of a national celebration burst from his television.

He could still feel it—nearly a decade after the first Obama election—when we spoke over the phone for the first time. Joselo told me he had never been particularly political; his thoughts were more occupied with his job at the dry cleaner than with America's increasingly bitter partisan politics. But it would have been impossible to miss the excitement of the 2008 campaign—he still remembers how it coursed through the nation like a fever chill. This moment, everyone around him seemed to insist, was different. It was important that he pay attention: America was about to elect a black president.

Joselo and his friends hoped that if their adopted country was willing to embrace such a massive, historic change, maybe it would be willing to consider some smaller ones too. "We could see it, we could see the change of the nation," Joselo would tell me later. "But also we were talking about how things were going to change on immigration. Everyone was so happy."

Maybe the politicians in Washington would finally come up with a plan that would allow his many undocumented friends—and his older brother, Marcelo—to come out of the shadows. Perhaps his coworkers and neighbors would finally shed the ever-present fear that, any day now, a chance encounter with a police officer or sheriff's deputy would leave them banished from their new home, dragged back to the violence and poverty they'd fled.

For that moment, on that night, Joselo Lucero believed that change had come to America. Or at least that's what he hoped.

When the Lucero brothers arrived in America in the early 2000s, they were entering a country deeply fearful of the droves of Central and South American immigrants who'd arrived in recent decades. The preceding half century had brought dynamic change to the nation, but parts of the American story remained unaltered.

Four decades earlier, in 1965, the country had fundamentally overhauled the way immigration works, doing away with a quota system based on nationality and installing a tiered visa system accompanied by an overall cap on the total number of immigrants allowed in each year. Immigration levels had been relatively stagnant for decades due to the strict limitations on how many migrants were permitted to enter the United States. Now those limitations were gone. "It was one of the most transformative laws in our nation's history," journalist Jia Lynn Yang writes of the Immigration and Nationality Act of 1965 in *One Mighty and Irresistible Tide: The Epic Struggle over American Immigration, 1924–1965*. "By ending a system of racial preferences among immigrants, the law reversed a decades-long decline in immigration levels and opened the door to Asian, Latin American, African, and Middle Eastern immigration at a scale never before seen—changes that are so evident now that they seem to have been inevitable."

The decades that followed these changes would see the number of immigrants as a proportion of the population increase to levels on par with those in the decades between the Civil War and World War I, when Italians and Jews were arriving en masse. While immigrants accounted for just 4.8 percent of the country's population in 1970, in 2018 they made up 13.7 percent, or 44.8 million people—the highest total in the nation's history.

The greatest factor in that change was an influx of Central and South American immigrants. There were fewer than one million Latino immigrants in the United States in 1960, but by 2010, that number would soar to nineteen million. First came a flow of Mexicans and Cubans. Then Colombians and Argentinians, Dominicans and Salvadorians. Guatemalans, Peruvians, and Ecuadorians like the Luceros. "Crippled by a mounting debt crisis, Ecuador began to export people instead of hats," journalist Mirta Ojito wrote of the surge of Ecuadorians into the United States in the 1980s and 1990s. "Unable to find jobs at home or elsewhere in their own country, thousands of Ecuadorians left for New York in whatever way it was possible: either legally, with a visa, or illegally, by crossing the border surreptitiously or buying fake visas. Everyone seemed to be migrating north or knew someone who had already left on the perilous and costly journey."

The vast majority of Latin American immigrants had come legally—through the byzantine visa process that often took years to successfully navigate—in order to fill vital agricultural and service jobs that powered the U.S. economy. Others trekked miles across rough terrain to cross the southern border illegally or overstayed their visas in order to access the jobs and safety offered here. Before long, the nation became obsessed with the ostensible threat of this "illegal" immigration.

In early 2005 the Republican congressman Jim Sensenbrenner of Wisconsin, chairman of the House Judiciary Committee, introduced the Border Protection, Antiterrorism and Illegal Immigration Control Act, which proposed increasing funding for more barriers along the border with Mexico, a faster process for deporting those in the country illegally, and stiffer fines for anyone who assisted an undocumented immigrant to enter or remain in the country. At the time, there were an estimated eleven million undocumented immigrants in the country, and politicians like Sensenbrenner feared that without decisive action, millions more would be on the way.

His legislation, Sensenbrenner explained to me years later, was an attempt at forcing compromise. He knew that his border security bill would pass in the House, while the Senate would be more likely to pass a more liberal bill. Then, he reasoned, the two chambers would be forced to land at a compromise somewhere in the middle.

For decades, Republicans and Democrats alike had known the nation's immigration system was not working. Entering the country legally often required laborious, complicated processes that could stretch on for years. Millions of people had instead crossed the border without documentation, living and working in the United States without legal status.

There had been attempts at reforming the immigration system in the past, but those efforts, in Sensenbrenner's mind, were too flimsy on border security—allowing new migrations of undocumented workers—and too lenient about granting citizenship status to those already in the country without documentation, thus encouraging future illegal immigration. "I decided to take a whack at it even though I knew this was kind of going into the lion's den, because to solve the problem would require a lot of compromise."

But his proposed legislation sparked widespread concern about mass deportations and prompted mobilization from immigrants' rights groups, setting in motion protests across the country. One hundred thousand people marched in Chicago, and a half million in Los Angeles. On May 1, 2006, both documented and undocumented immigrants across the country staged "Day Without an Immigrant," during which instead of working, they took to the streets again. "The only political avenue that we had available to us was to take to the politics of the street," Armando Navarro, a longtime immigrants' rights advocate, recalled a decade later. "We had to show our power; our capability manifested by our numbers."

As the street protest raged, Senators Ted Kennedy (D-Massachusetts) and John McCain (R-Arizona) seized the moment to press for a comprehensive overhaul to the nation's immigration system, introducing legislation that would have allowed the seven million undocumented immigrants who had been in the country for five or more years to apply for citizenship by paying a fine and any back taxes they owed. Another three million undocumented residents would be eligible to apply for work visas. On the political Left, some labor unions worried that the increase in work visas would flood the labor market with immigrant workers who would compete with their members. On the political Right, the idea that those who had entered the country illegally—and thus broken the law—would be granted "amnesty" and allowed to become citizens deeply offended conservative law-and-order sensibilities. Senator Jeff Sessions of Alabama, one of the legislation's chief Republican opponents, proclaimed on the Senate floor: "The American people are not against immigration. They are worried about a system that is lawless, unprincipled, and, indeed, makes a mockery of law. And they have every right to be so. We should not give those who violate our laws to get here every single right we give the people who wait in line and come lawfully."

The Secure America and Orderly Immigration Act earned Senate passage but ultimately failed after House Republicans refused to enter a conference to resolve the differences between the bills. McCain and Senate Democrats attempted again the following year but couldn't get a vote to pass even the upper chamber.

The firestorm that had been kicked up on the political Right would remain unextinguished for the next decade and a half. "Amnesty" and "border security" remained two of the most mobilizing issues among the Republican Party's majority white electoral base—with partisan conservative media eagerly fanning the flames. To understand this pivotal turn in the public discourse is to understand much of the decade of American politics that followed.

"What surprised us was this backlash," said Frank Sharry, executive director of America's Voice, which advocates for a pathway to citizenship for undocumented immigrants, and a longtime advocate on behalf of immigrants' rights in Washington. "All of these mostly Latino families, dressed in white, carrying American flags and saying, 'We want to be Americans,' were so threatening to Middle America," he said. "Whoa, we didn't see that coming."

Chief among those sounding the alarm was Lou Dobbs, a prime-time CNN news anchor who was then one of the most powerful media voices in the country. In 2006 the *New York Times* described him as "the nation's most prominent opponent of current immigration policy," noting that he had taken to the airwaves to declare the Senate reform bill "an unconscionable act" and "a sellout," and that "illegal immigrants are a burden to the taxpayer, unequivocally." In the years to come, Dobbs would claim falsely that the borders were "demonstrably wide open," and that the proposed guest worker program was "opposed by the majority of Americans." In one television segment, which raised alarms that undocumented immigrants were carrying diseases into the United States, one of Dobbs's correspondents asserted that in the past three years the country had seen seven thousand cases of leprosy—up from nine hundred cases over the last forty years. "Incredible," Dobbs responded.

That was not true. The report being cited actually showed that there had been seven thousand leprosy cases over the previous *thirty* years, and that it was unclear what, if any, connection such cases had to undocumented immigrants. When veteran correspondent Lesley Stahl challenged the clear error on *60 Minutes*, Dobbs responded by declaring, "If we reported it, it's a fact."

For the next decade, the terms "broken borders," "amnesty," and "illegals" were laundered into the American discourse via Dobbs's six o'clock evening news hour. (In 2010 Dobbs would find a new home on the conservative Fox News Channel, where he continued to champion the racist "birther" conspiracy theory, which suggested baselessly that Barack Obama was not born in the United States and therefore was ineligible to serve as president.)

Dobbs was far from alone. Similar rhetoric was a mainstay of conservative talk radio. "We've now traded liberty for perversity," Rush Limbaugh proclaimed in a 2007 radio segment, typical of his show at the time. "America is being erased, in the sense that the distinct American culture is being erased because we don't have the guts to stand up for it like we did in the past when it came to massive numbers of immigrants." Fox News, where conservative commentators enjoyed wide latitude to spout factually dubious claims about immigrants without fear of on-air pushback much less behind the scenes sanction, would go on to become the most-watched cable network in the nation and the most powerful force in American politics. Bill O'Reilly, then its popular evening opinion host, used his program to highlight crimes allegedly committed by undocumented immigrants. In 2006 Pat Buchanan, a Fox News regular and former White House aide to Richard Nixon, published his bestselling *State of Emergency: The Third World Invasion and Conquest of America*, which warned ominously, "This is an invasion, the greatest invasion in history."

By the 2006 midterm elections, immigration was considered a political "wedge" issue. Republicans blasted Senator Maria Cantwell (D-Washington) for her vote against an amendment that the GOP had attempted to attach to the immigration reform bill that would have banned undocumented immigrants from collecting Social Security benefits for wages earned while in the country illegally. Ultimately, Cantwell held on to her seat. In an Illinois congressional race, Republican Peter Roskam sent out a mailer attacking his Democratic opponent, Tammy Duckworth, for her support of the McCain-Kennedy bill, claiming that it amounted to—here's that word again—"amnesty for illegal aliens." His campaign would go on to describe her and her views on immigration as "unhinged." Ultimately, Roskam won the election by 4,810 votes.

"It was at a time when the people who were most afraid of immigrants lived in communities with very few immigrants or where immigrants were just arriving," Sharry told me. "People were sending bricks—build the wall—to their members of Congress."

This backlash was playing out not just in the headlines and halls of Congress, but also in communities such as Patchogue, where the Lucero brothers had settled.

As Mirta Ojito documents in her book *Hunting Season: Immigration and Murder in an All-American Town*, white outrage at the Latino arrivals soon took over politics and policy in parts of Long Island, where historically white communities had seen an influx of Latino immigrants. In 2001 Michael M. D'Andre, a legislator from Smithtown, declared at a public hearing that if his town observed a notable spike in day laborers, "we'll be out with baseball bats," while in 2006 a school board member in the Hamptons circulated a petition to prevent undocumented children from receiving "free services." And in 2007 Elie Mystal, a legislator from Amityville, declared that if he spotted day laborers gathered in his community, "I would load my gun and start shooting, period."

This animus came at what was unquestionably a time of economic anxiety for many Americans, especially in the middle- and working-class enclaves in places such as Long Island. Beginning in late 2007, the country entered the worst economic downturn since the Great Depression. And the Great Recession, as it came to be known, arrived amid an already weakened job market and on the heels of a decade in which middle-class families had seen their net income fall, after factoring in inflation.

In Suffolk County, which encompasses most of Long Island, residents voiced concerns that the wave of migrant workers would depress property values, prompting additional vows from white elected officials that they would not allow their communities to be overrun by immigrant day laborers who shared homes and crowded city streets each morning awaiting someone to pick them up for a gig. "People who play by the rules work hard to achieve the suburban dream of the white picket fence," Suffolk County executive Steve Levy told the *New York Times* in 2007. "If you live in the suburbs, you do not want to live across the street from a house where sixty men live. You do not want trucks riding up and down the block at five a.m. picking up workers." In Patchogue, an assumption spread that the true reason behind a recent round of school athletics cuts was due to the district's need to pay for English-as-second-language courses for immigrant children, who in five years had gone from making up 4 percent of students to 24 percent.

There was more than just tough talk: across the county, immigrants had reported being targeted by groups of white teenagers, who would drive up to them, shouting slurs and throwing rocks. Sometimes these groups would jump unsuspecting Latino men on the street—"beaner hopping," they called it. National hate crime data from the years leading up to Barack Obama's election show a clear trend: a 40 percent uptick in targeted attacks against Latinos from 2003 to 2007.

While Marcelo loved his new country, so much that he hung an American flag across the wall of his living room, he surmised quickly that his new home didn't always love people like him and his brother. Immigrant men would exchange stories of harassment as they talked outside the local laundromat on Saturdays. One of the brothers' close friends got pulled over by police so many times that he refused to drive his own car anymore. They'd escaped the violence of their birth countries, but knew danger still lurked all around.

Marcelo, thirty-seven, had always been like a father to his younger siblings. Their real father had died when they were young, so it fell to him to help his mom keep the family afloat. He'd facilitated his younger brother's move to New York, in part so that Joselo could avoid having to fight in Ecuador's ongoing military conflict with Peru.

Their apartments sat just a few hundred feet from each other— Marcelo could look out his window and see if Joselo's car was in its usual parking spot. If he glanced out late at night and didn't spot it, he'd call. "Where are you? What are you up to?" he'd pester his younger brother. "Stay out of trouble."

Joselo chuckles now, as he remembers their conversations: They would reminisce about the world they had grown up in and swapped remedies for the struggles of surviving the world they now occupied. Memories of how poor they once were. Boasts about how far they'd made it. Fantasies of even better days to come.

The last time Joselo saw his older brother was the Friday night after the election. His voice still goes quiet as he recalls it. They were at a home near the train station, where an Ecuadorian woman who'd taken on the role of community cook would supply an end-less stream of immigrant workers with unlimited plates in exchange for a donation of a few dollars. The Luceros had made a habit of meeting there after work, catching up while eating their fill, and then walking the handful of blocks home.

A few nights later, Marcelo Lucero was dead.

THE QUESTION OF WHO, EXACTLY, is entitled to live here has defined much of American history since the colonists excised the Native populations from their land and successfully earned their independence by defeating Britain in the Revolutionary War. For nearly a century, the young nation debated whether to end the brutal institution of slavery, which had imported millions of black men, women, and children like cattle, held them in bondage, and denied them family, autonomy, and citizenship. Even following the emancipation of black people, among the fundamental questions facing the country in the century to come would be which, if any, of the waves of new immigrants would be allowed in when they showed up on American shores.

Beginning in the 1920s, legislators began passing strict immigration quotas limiting how many people of each nationality could enter. (By then, another series of laws had already banned immigration from most of Asia and made a point to exclude Chinese immigrants specifically.) The 1924 Immigration Act, for example, set the cap on the total number of immigrants who could come here at 165,000 annually. It also applied a quota for each nationality: equal to 2 percent of the number of Americans of that nationality as of the 1890 census. Naturally these laws favored immigrants from northern and Western Europe (the British, the Germans, the Irish), who already made up significant chunks of the U.S. population. The laws also limited the number of new Catholic and Jewish immigrants who could arrive from Eastern and southern Europe. These limits were driven, as much as anything, by fear.

Historian Erika Lee, in her introduction to *America for Americans: A History of Xenophobia in the United States*, writes, "Americans have been wary of almost every group of foreigners that has come to the United States: German immigrants in the eighteenth century; Irish and Chinese in the nineteenth century; Italians, Jews, Japanese, and Mexicans in the twentieth century; and Muslims today." She goes on to say, "History shows that xenophobia has been a constant and defining feature of American life," adding, "Even as Americans have realized that the threats allegedly posed by immigrants were, in hindsight, unjustified, they have allowed xenophobia to become an American tradition."

Xenophobia can be broadly defined as a fear, skepticism, or hatred of foreigners. Much like other forms of racism, it manifests both as interpersonal prejudice and as a form of systemic discrimination—wielded against whichever group is currently considered a threat. And, as Lee documents, the dark force of xenophobia has been ever-present in American society.

A similar script played out through two centuries of American history: a new group of immigrants shows up, their arrival prompts outrage and panic. Coarse, inflammatory political rhetoric—driven by derogatory racial stereotypes, which it then reinforces—is accompanied by new restrictions and limitations aimed at excluding and repressing the new population. The citizenry, convinced that these immigrants present a unique threat to their way of life, lashes out violently. This is the American Whitelash.

By the time of the Rock Springs Massacre in 1885, Chinese immigrants had been working in U.S. mines for nearly four decades, having arrived amid the California Gold Rush of 1849. Chinese workers were farming in countless American fields and contributed significantly to the building of the transcontinental railroad across the West.

In Wyoming, the financially strapped Union Pacific had begun cutting miners' pay, resulting in workers' strikes that, in turn, prompted the railroad to begin importing cheap immigrant laborers. Even at the reduced rates, Chinese workers could earn several times the salary they would have found in China, and because many of the workers had left their families behind, they'd room together, sometimes with more than a half dozen men to a home, saving on housing costs. By 1885, there were six hundred Chinese miners working the mines in Rock Springs, a mining town near the southwestern corner of the state, double the number of white miners.

Though their true conflict was with the well-off white men who owned and operated the railway and refused to pay a fair wage, the white miners began to aim their vitriol at the immigrants. The willingness of these Chinese migrants to work for cheap, the white miners reasoned, was depressing everyone's wages. Each employed Chinese worker, they reasoned, was stealing a livelihood to which they were entitled.

Throughout that summer, there had been reports of Chinese men being threatened or beaten in Cheyenne, Laramie, and Rawlins. "It is said that the mine bosses have favored the Chinamen to the detriment of white miners, and it needed only a spark to kindle the flames," the *New-York Times* wrote at the time. On the morning of September 2 a fight broke out between white and Chinese workers in Rock Springs. The brawl left one Chinese miner dead and several others badly beaten. That was the spark. By noon, a white mob had descended on the section of town where the Chinese workers lived and burned it to the ground, leaving about two dozen Chinese immigrants dead. This was the scene, per the *Times*:

After dinner, the saloons closed and no liquor has since been sold. The miners gathered on the front streets, about 100 of

them armed with guns, revolvers, hatchets, and knives, and proceeded toward Chinatown. Before reaching there they sent a
committee of three to warn the Chinamen to leave in an hour.
This they agreed to do, and started to pack up, but in about half
an hour, the white men became impatient and advanced upon
the Chinese quarters, shouting and firing their guns into the
air. Without offering resistance, the Chinese fled with whatever
they could snatch up. They fled to the hills about a mile east
of the town, the miners firing at them as they fled. The miners
then set fire to some of the houses, and soon eight or ten of
the largest houses were in flames. Half choked with fire and
smoke, numbers of Chinamen came rushing from the burning buildings, and, with blankets and quilts over their heads to
protect themselves from stray rifle shots, they followed their
retreating brothers into the hills at the top of their speed.

When Governor Francis E. Warren traveled to Rock Springs
the following day to calm the unrest, the white miners demanded
(successfully) that no one be arrested for the violence and (unsuccessfully) that no Chinese immigrants ever be allowed to live there
again.

Just six years later, white Americans were again lashing out violently at a group of recently arrived immigrants. On March 14,
1891, a mob of thousands stormed a New Orleans jail en route to
carrying out the deadliest lynching in U.S. history.

As the historian John V. Baiamonte Jr. notes, at the time much of
the French Quarter was heavily populated with Sicilians who had
immigrated in droves to fill the demand for cheap labor left behind
by the abolition of slavery. The area had a reputation for being
violent, with one stretch of Decatur Street so known for shootings
and stabbings that it was called "Vendetta Alley." It soon became
accepted—without evidence—that the Italian Mafia was responsible for the area's crime problem.

While today we'd understand Italian Americans as "white," in the 1890s the immigrants arriving in New Orleans were certainly not considered so. Races, we know, are socially constructed classifications, not hardwired biological distinctions. As the journalist Brent Staples of the *New York Times* writes, "[R]acial categories that people mistakenly view as matters of biology grow out of highly politicized myth making." Italian American journalist Joe Ragazzo adds, "Italians in America have benefited from a decades-long societal evolution where we have come to be seen as 'white.' It shouldn't matter if a group of people is white or not, but it's undeniable that it does matter."

But before we can understand the importance of whiteness and how a group secures it, we must grapple with how American whiteness was created in the first place.

"The discovery of personal whiteness among the world's people is a very modern thing—a nineteenth and twentieth century matter, indeed," the sociologist and author W. E. B. Du Bois writes in his 1920 essay "The Souls of White Folk." "The ancient world would have laughed at such a distinction. The Middle Ages regarded skin color with mild curiosity; and even up into the eighteenth century we were hammering our national manikins into one, great, Universal Man, with fine frenzy which ignored color and race even more than birth. Today we have changed all that, and the world in a sudden, emotional conversion has discovered that it is white and by that token, wonderful!"

Scholar Ibram X. Kendi, in his National Book Award–winning *Stamped from the Beginning: A Definitive History of Racist Ideas* (2016), documents that, in the American context, the concept of race—and thus American racism as we understand it—has developed in a way counterintuitive to what most of us assume. Kendi defines a "racist idea" as any idea that assumes one racial group is innately inferior or innately superior to another racial group. In essence, the very belief in biological races—the idea advanced from the eugenicists, to the anti-Semites, to some modern political commentators that there are biologically distinct black people and white people, who are born fundamentally different from one another—is itself racist. Racist ideas, because they are just that—ideas—can be held, perpetuated by, and acted upon by people of any race.

What Kendi shows in *Stamped* is the extent to which racist ideas—specifically antiblack racist ideas such as the belief in black subhumanity, intellectual inferiority, or inclination to violence—sprout not due to bigotry but rather as convenient tools to explain away an already unjust status quo or in the pursuit of public policy that would further that inequality. "Time and again, racist ideas have not been cooked up from the boiling pot of ignorance and hate," Kendi writes. "Time and again, powerful and brilliant men and women have produced racist ideas in order to justify the racist policies of their era, in order to redirect the blame for their era's racial disparities away from those policies and onto black people." In other words, faced with the reality that black people are mistreated and that those in power benefit from that ongoing mistreatment, it is not only easier but *advantageous* to blame the black people—to invent an ideological pseudoscience suggesting that black people must be inherently inferior—than it is to take the public policy steps required to correct the inequality.

The first permanent English settlement in North America was Jamestown, Virginia, founded in 1607. A dozen years later, in 1619, the first recorded shipment of enslaved Africans arrived at a port nearby. During those early decades, much of the labor that supported the colonies was conducted by slaves and indentured servants—both African and British—who had the opportunity to eventually purchase their freedom in addition to slave labor. "When the first Africans arrived in Virginia in 1619, there were no 'white' people there; nor, according to the colonial records, would there be for another sixty years," writes the historian Theodore W. Allen in his two-volume book *The Invention of the White Race*, published in the mid-1990s.

Allen notes that the first appearance of the term *white* in Virginia law came in 1691, after a series of working-class rebellions, including, most infamously, Bacon's Rebellion in 1676—during which white and black laborers had banded together against the colonial governor—had upended the colony. The legal invention of race, he theorizes, served as a means of undermining class solidarity between the British indentured servants and the African servants and slaves they labored alongside. By convincing working-class British colonists that their fates were not linked to those of the African workers but instead to the landowners who largely ran the Virginia colony, the powerful could ensure that they were not overthrown.

"Race supplied the key to resolving these conflicts," writes the historian James D. Rice. "Simply put, ordinary planters agreed to accept the rule of their elite superiors, while the gentry agreed to treat common planters and white servants more respectfully. And together, both sorts agreed to share the benefits of white supremacy. . . . Thus, the codification of Virginia law culminating in 1705 drew a stark line between whites and everyone else, making it possible for those on the right side of that line to enjoy greater liberty and equality while also benefiting from the fruits of slavery. . . .

"The implications of this new social order penetrated into almost every part of life," Rice continues. "Racial slavery and white populism—white tribalism, one might say—forced Indians and Africans to shoulder the burden of resolving the tensions and divisions within colonial society. Now a slave's every gesture and word were examined by whites for signs that racial discipline was being observed. As the slave population increased, even the poorest, unhappiest white Virginians were lifted further from the bottom of society."

In his 1949 book *Jesus and the Disinherited*, theologian Howard Thurman writes that oppressed minority groups face two options: they can either assimilate or they can resist. "Under the general plan of nonresistance, one may take the position of imitation. The aim of such an attitude is to assimilate the culture and the social behavior-pattern of the dominant group. It is the profound capitulation to the powerful, because it means the yielding of oneself to that which, deep within, one recognizes as being unworthy. It makes for a strategic loss of self-respect. The aim is to reduce all outer or external designs of difference to zero, so that there shall be no ostensible cause for active violence or oppression."

The Italians, like other immigrant groups before and after them, would spend decades working to assimilate into American whiteness. And as a result, American whiteness, over time, has expanded to accommodate waves of new members—a process currently underway with many of the Central and South American immigrants who have arrived in recent years.

But, at the time, Italians, especially Sicilians, were considered, by decree of the white supremacist hierarchy, functionally black. And we know there are few things more dangerous than being black in America—a status that confers suspicion, ill will, and contempt. To be black is to not belong, to be viewed as less than fully citizen and less than fully human, to be excluded from democracy's spoils while blamed for its ills. "Because Southern Italians, in particular, often had a dark complexion and shiny black hair, many Anglos questioned their membership in the 'white race,'" historian Manfred Berg writes in *Popular Justice: A History of Lynching in America*. "According to prevailing ideas of 'racial purity,' their ambiguous skin color signaled a sinister character and a proclivity for crime."

Those perceptions hardened in New Orleans after a May 1890 shooting between members of two Italian families, the Matrangas and the Provenzanos. The incident was apparently sparked by a dispute over who controlled fruit-unloading docks on the waterfront. Two members of the Matranga family and four others had been ambushed and shot, allegedly by two members of the Provenzano family. As the trial neared, the incident was "portrayed by the press and later writers as the beginning of a Mafia war," John Baiamonte writes. "Although the state prosecutor did not allege that the Mafia was involved in the Provenzano-Matranga feud, he did charge that the Sicilian vendetta plagued New Orleans." He adds: "Ironically, all public references to the Mafia involvement in the Provenzano-Matranga case came from the press . . . and not law enforcement officials."

By the time New Orleans Police Chief David C. Hennessy began his walk home from the station around eleven o'clock on the night of October 15, 1890, the Provenzanos had been convicted, filed an appeal, and were awaiting a second trial in just a matter of days. As Baiamonte writes:

> It was rumored that Hennessey would testify with new evidence on behalf of . . . the Provenzanos. Probably with thoughts of the upcoming trial on his mind, Hennessey parted with his friend [police Captain Bill] O'Connor. He continued to walk toward his home, but he never arrived. Out of the darkness came a barrage of gunfire. Hennessey drew his revolver and fired on his assassins as he attempted to chase them near Girod and Lafayette streets. When O'Connor and others reached the mortally wounded chief, he allegedly whispered "The dagoes did it."

Those four inflammatory words—"The dagoes did it"—would set in motion a series of events that ended in massacre.

Mayor Joseph Shakspeare declared the chief a "victim of Sicilian vengeance" and ordered the police to search the city's Italian neighborhoods. Within hours, five dozen Italian men had been arrested in connection with the chief's death. The raids on Italian homes and meeting places continued for days. City officials released a list of ninety-four murders supposedly committed by Italians—the roster including killings dating back more than two decades. Some of the perpetrators were not, in fact, Italian, but the document nonetheless advanced the perception that Italian immigrants were predisposed to violence and criminality. The local press, in both editorials and articles, referred to the chief's "dago assassins" and warned that the Mafia may have been on the verge of taking over the city. Ultimately, nine Italian men were sent to trial. But in the absence of any legitimate evidence tying the men to the crime, six were acquitted, and the other three saw their cases end in mistrials. Those men were thrown back in jail to await trial on additional charges.

Much of the city's white citizenry was enraged, convinced that the verdicts were an abdication of justice. The local papers carried an announcement for a mass meeting at ten o'clock on the morning of March 14, 1891. Thousands showed up—mostly white, although attendees reportedly included at least a few black people—and after fiery speeches, the crowd-turned-mob stormed the jailhouse, ramming their way through the back entrance.

Baiamonte writes: "The guards did not fire on the mob. Some actually turned over their weapons. On a tip from some of the guards, a squad entered the women's section and chased six Italians, who had been released by the warden, into a locked stairway. As the Sicilians huddled in fear, the group fired more than a hundred rifle shots and shotgun blasts. Their bodies were riddled mercilessly. This was followed by laughter and cheers, but some turned away in disgust."

By the rampage's end, eleven Italians had been shot or lynched. As the names of the dead were read aloud, the assembled crowd cheered.

The slain victims were further vilified by the press, denied dignity even in death. The editorial board of the *New-York Times* disparaged them as "sneaking and cowardly Sicilians, the descendants of bandits and assassins, who have transported to this country the lawless passions, the cut-throat practices, and the oath-bound societies of their native country." The headline for the *Washington Post*'s news story about the lynchings framed the killings as "vengeance." According to the article, "The Mafia has been struck a death blow. . . . Last night a body of cool-headed men, lawyers, doctors, merchants, and political leaders, all persons of influence and social standing, quietly met and decided that some action must be taken, and the people's justice, swift and sure, visited upon those who the jury had neglected to punish."

Theodore Roosevelt—then a member of the U.S. Civil Service Commission and later the New York City police commissioner, assistant secretary of the U.S. Navy, governor of New York, vice president, and then two-term president of the United States—reflected the bigotry and callousness felt toward the Italian lynching victims by many Americans. "Monday we dined at the Camerons; various dago diplomats were present, all much wrought up by the lynching of the Italians in New Orleans," he wrote in a March 21, 1891, letter to his sister Anna. "Personally I think it rather a good thing, and said so."

But the lynchings in New Orleans would ultimately accelerate the process by which Italian Americans became "white." The Italian government, outraged at the killings, broke off diplomatic relations with the United States. As part of his attempt to repair that bridge, President Benjamin Harrison established Columbus Day and began the mythologizing that would for more than a century to come cast Italians as among the first Americans.

"Harrison's Columbus Day proclamation in 1892 opened the door for Italian Americans to write themselves into the American origin story, in a fashion that piled myth upon myth," Staples writes in the *New York Times*. "They rewrote history by casting Columbus as 'the first immigrant'—even though he never set foot in North America and never immigrated anywhere (except possibly to Spain). . . . It also tied Italian Americans closely to the paternalistic assertion, still heard today, that Columbus 'discovered' a continent that was already inhabited by Native Americans."

In other words, the myth of Christopher Columbus's "discovery" was enough to make Italians white.

The U.S. government agreed to pay reparations to the Italian American lynching victims, cutting a check for $25,000 total to be distributed among the families of three of the victims. The lynchings remain one of the darkest moments in the history of the Italian American experience. In April 2019, nearly 130 years later, New Orleans mayor LaToya Cantrell, the first black woman to hold the office, issued an official apology.

"What happened to those eleven Italians, it was wrong, and the city owes them and their descendants a formal apology. At this late date, we cannot give justice. But we can be intentional and deliberate about what we do going forward," she said. "This attack was an act of anti-immigrant violence."

This cycle would continue, an ugly song stuck on repeat, for the next 125 years. Pick any immigrant group, and its members can recount—often with not only historical examples but also contemporary anecdotes—episodes of ostracism, discrimination, and violence that its people have faced upon arriving in the United States. The details and locations differ, but the chorus remains the same.

Hundreds of white men stalked the streets of Watsonville, California, for five days in January 1930, attacking Filipino men who they believed had come to steal their jobs and their women.

A twenty-two-year-old man named Fermin Tobera was shot and killed by the rioters, yet his slaying was never prosecuted. Thirteen years later, white U.S. Navy sailors tore through downtown Los Angeles for ten days attacking Mexican Americans in what became known as the "Zoot Suit Riots." Even in the face of such violence, it was the victims—not the attackers—who were defamed by the media. As the *Los Angeles Times* noted in a 2020 apology for decades of coverage that fueled racial animus and violence:

> The *Times* largely ignored the context—the social and economic upheaval brought about by wartime mobilization and the racist trope of threatened white womanhood—and blamed the victims instead of their assailants. When First Lady Eleanor Roosevelt suggested that the rioting might have grown out of racial discrimination toward Mexican Americans, the *Times* vehemently denied that was possible, asserting in an editorial, "We like Mexicans, and we think they like us."

Even decades later, in post–civil rights America, it was more of the same. In August 1984 a riot broke out in Lawrence, Massachusetts, after members of a white family hurled a brick through the window of a home in Lower Tower Hill, where a number of Dominican and Puerto Rican immigrants had settled. "It had to come," an older white businessman told a *New York Times* reporter in the wake of the violence. "This used to be a good city, but you get all these Spanish people in here, and ninety percent of them don't work. I think they're pushy people." Four years later, in 1988, a twenty-eight-year-old Ethiopian student named Mulugeta Seraw was beaten to death by a group of white skinheads in Portland, prompting Oregon to pass the nation's first hate crime law.

This xenophobic hostility has not been reserved solely for those who've come recently, but also to those brought here forcibly long ago. As waves of emancipated black Americans fled the Jim Crow

South and began arriving in northern and western cities—a relo-cation, known as the Great Migration, that stretched from 1915 to 1970—they were treated as unwelcome immigrants in what had been for most of them the nation of their birth.

"Over the course of six decades, some six million black south-erners left the land of their forefathers and fanned out across the country for an uncertain existence in nearly every other corner of America," the Pulitzer Prize–winning journalist and author Isabel Wilkerson writes in *The Warmth of Other Suns: The Epic Story of America's Great Migration.* "From the moment the emigrants set foot in the North and West, they were blamed for the troubles of the cities they fled to."

There were lynchings, torched homes, and angry white mobs who took to the street in opposition to the suggestion they share communities, jobs, and schools with their new black neighbors. That was the case in Chicago, where the city's black population doubled between 1915 and 1920. What followed was American Whitelash.

"Almost overnight, the South Side emerged as a social, cultural, and institutional center for African Americans. That community would gestate modern blues, soul, and gospel; landmark mass-market journalism; the largest black Protestant and nationalist churches; and, in time, the first black president," writes the histo-rian Adam Green. In 1919, though, the South Side's demographic revolution was seen by white locals mainly as a threat.

On July 27, a seventeen-year-old black boy named Eugene Wil-liams was swimming off the beach of Lake Michigan when the raft he was riding on drifted over the de facto line separating the black and white sections of Twenty-Ninth Street Beach. An enraged white beachgoer reportedly began throwing rocks at Williams and the other black kids who were in the water, and Williams slipped off his raft and drowned. The responding police declined to arrest the white man who had thrown the rocks, enraging the black youths who'd gathered. One black beachgoer pulled out a pistol, and the police responded by shooting him dead.

As word of the incident spread throughout the city, bands of angry white men piled into cars, drove into black neighborhoods, and opened fire on homes and businesses. Others marched up and down city streets, assaulting black residents at random, at times pulling them off streetcars. The violence continued for thirteen days, resulting in thirty-eight deaths, more than five hundred injuries, and a thousand homeless families.

The Negro in Chicago, a 1922 report commissioned following the riot, concluded, "The relation of whites and Negroes in the United States is our most grave and perplexing domestic problem." More than four decades later, Martin Luther King Jr. and other civil rights leaders came to Chicago to join local activists in demonstrating against racial segregation in housing, employment, and education—a system that kept black people living in slum neighborhoods, stuck in low-paying jobs, and attending failing schools. Upon their arrival, they were met by a riotous white crowd that pelted them with bottles and bricks. "I have seen many demonstrations in the South, but I have never seen anything so hostile and so hateful as I've seen here today," King remarked. To this day, much of the racial geography of Chicago, and many other American cities, can be traced back directly to this era of American Whitelash, when many white residents fled urban centers for the suburbs due to the influx of black migrants.

All of this violence—attacks on the Chinese, the Italians, and the black Americans who had been unwillingly imported—was definitionally white supremacy at work: carried out in defense of the established racial order in which those deemed white were the only true citizens, entitled to America's bounty and liberty and without any obligation to share. Their rage was in defense of whiteness from a perceived threat. As beneficiaries of an unjust system, they were determined to preserve a discriminatory status quo that worked in their favor.

The violence was often not only excused but also explicitly encouraged by powerful, white-run institutions: elected officials, neighborhood and business councils, and the press. Through the misleading deployment of statistics and forthright expressions of bigotry, these entities further solidified stereotypes about dirty, poor, violent, job-stealing, fornicating "others."

6

THE ORIGINAL TEENAGE TRIO IN Patchogue had met up early in the evening to go beaner hopping. They started out in Farmingville, five miles north, but couldn't find any immigrants to harass there. So, after stealing a few lawn ornaments, they made their way to Patchogue, where they confronted a Hispanic man who was out on his front porch; he chased them off with a beer bottle. Deterred, at least for the moment, they picked up a case of Budweiser and met up with several others friends, including Jeff Conroy, at a nearby train station. On the way there, they'd pulled over on the side of the road to attack an intoxicated Hispanic man they'd spotted walking with his bike—punching and kicking him, calling him names, and snatching his baseball cap as a trophy.

The next few hours were spent hanging out at the station. Some of the dozen or so teenage boys and girls sipped warm beers. One boy shot at a ticket machine with a BB gun he'd been carrying around. From there, they all headed over to a nearby park, where groups of two and three people wandered around gossiping.

After a while, they decided to get back to violence. One of the boys suggested they leave the park and go "fuck up some Mexicans." None of the girls were interested, but seven boys piled into a car and set out into the night. They spotted a man who appeared to be Hispanic walking down the street. Someone shouted that they should stop the car. Four of the boys jumped out and ran toward him. Soon they were committing their second attack of the night.

The man in their sights was fifty-seven-year-old Hector Sierra, who'd just finished a double shift at a nearby Colombian restaurant, where he was the head waiter. A few of Sierra's friends had previously told him about their experiences being jumped by white teenagers. So, when he saw the group headed his way, he immediately began to run. But the teens were faster.

"They caught me from behind, they started punching me and kicking me from behind, punching me on my ears. . . . I was really running for my life, you know," Sierra would later testify in court. He broke away from them and stumbled up to a nearby home and frantically hammered the door with his fist. "I was pounding on the window, and then I was kicking the door pretty hard. I feel embarrassed for that. But I was really pretty scared," Sierra said. When the porch light finally flicked on, the teenagers dashed back toward their car.

They drove a few blocks before parking and setting out on foot. Soon they spotted their next target: two Hispanic-looking men walking near the train station.

Criminologists and researchers who study racial violence believe the perpetrators of hate crimes, both race based and otherwise, generally fit one of three archetypes: thrill seekers, such as teenagers who paint swastikas on lockers or carve epithets into trees in order to bask in the glory of having done something edgy; reactive attackers, who lash out suddenly at perceived enemies such as immigrants or LGBTQ people; and mission-oriented attackers, the avowed ideologues who carry out calculated attacks in order to send a specific message or in pursuit of specific political ends.

The third group is unquestionably the most sinister: from Dylann Roof in Charleston to throngs of white supremacists in Charlottesville. But it is also the group most extensively monitored by law enforcement and the easiest to disrupt, if met with the appropriate effort. The thrill-seeking and reactive attackers, on the other hand, present a unique challenge to law enforcement and society as a whole. Their violence is less premeditated. Their motivations are rarely a fully articulated ideology. Instead, their actions are more impulsive, sudden overflows of grievance and hate.

And in America, the white supremacist movement has gone to great lengths in recent decades to stoke such outbursts. The movement hopes a barrage of messaging, laundered through mainstream politics and the media—such as dire warnings of a looming majority-minority America populated by brown immigrants and Muslims and moral panics about a culture taken over by black Americans and sexual deviants from gays and lesbians to transgender people—will spur not only their devoted followers but also average white Americans into violent action.

"This struggle is rapidly becoming a matter of individual action, each of its participants making a private decision in the quietness of his heart . . . to resist by any means necessary," Louis Beam Jr., one of the most prominent white supremacist leaders of the last half century, writes in his influential essay "Leaderless Resistance," which was published in 1992. Beam argues that the future of the movement lies in the actions of individuals, not bureaucratic organizations that could easily be infiltrated and disrupted by law enforcement.

"Organs of information distribution such as newspapers, leaflets, computers, etc., which are widely available to all, keep each person informed of events, allowing for a planned response that will take many variations. No one need issue an order to anyone," Beam continues. "Those idealists truly committed to the cause of freedom will act when they feel the time is ripe or will take their cue from others who precede them. . . . Let the coming night be filled with a thousand points of resistance."

On November 8, 2008, Long Island was one such point of resistance. While the Lucero brothers fantasized about an America in which they'd be safe from harassment, a group of teenagers drove through the village of Patchogue. Before long, they had Marcelo Lucero in their sights. Night had fallen, and horror had arrived.

Marcelo had spent the night drinking with Angel Loja, whom he'd known since they were young boys in Ecuador. Late in the evening, the men had decided to head to a house near the train tracks where another buddy lived. Normally, they would have driven. But Marcelo was a few drinks in and too responsible to risk getting behind the wheel. So, the men set off on foot. Their friend's house was in sight, just two or three doors away, when suddenly they were surrounded by seven teenagers.

The stories told later by the boys vary in detail, but the overarching shared narrative is that one of them drew in close to Lucero and Loja, shouted heated words and racial slurs, and then sucker punched Loja in the face. As Angel began to run, Marcelo took off his belt and began swinging it to defend himself from the various boys. That's when Jeff Conroy pulled out his knife and stabbed Lucero in the chest before the boys all took off running.

The young criminals didn't have much of an escape plan as they worked their way up the block. One boy told Conroy to ditch the knife, but he assured them he'd washed it off in a puddle to rid it of Marcelo's blood. They didn't make it very far—just a few blocks—before a police officer who was responding to a 911 call about the stabbing spotted the group and ordered them up against a wall.

Officers began searching and questioning the boys one at a time. Conroy stood near the end of the line, fidgeting nervously. Before long, he motioned to an officer and asked to speak with him, so the two walked together to the nearby curb.

"I have a blade on me," Conroy admitted, directing the officer to the black folding knife tucked in his waistband. "There's blood on this!" the policeman exclaimed as he examined the knife. Only later would the officers note the blood spots dotting the leg of Conroy's pants.

Conroy paused for a moment before offering a confession: "I stabbed him."

The first thing Pat Young saw when he arrived at the crime scene the following morning was a smear of blood drying on the asphalt.

He'd spent the weekend up near Boston with some college buddies, watching the New England Patriots take on their team, the Buffalo Bills. He'd made it most of the way back home that Sunday evening when he stopped for pizza at Frank Pepe's, his favorite spot in New Haven. Young heard a troubling report on news radio WCBS 880: a Latino immigrant had been stabbed to death in Patchogue. There were few other details in the report. That was it.

"I'm calling every freaking person on Long Island," Young would recount to me when we spoke years later. "No one would tell me, no one knew, exactly what happened. But they said it had been a group of young men. And, at this point, I guess that this could have been a hate crime."

Young had grown up in the area before heading off to the State University of New York at Buffalo. There his interest in human rights issues was first sparked when a Nicaraguan classmate, Jorge, was arrested by the autocratic regime of corrupt dictator Anastasio Somoza Debayle while back home during a school break. A week before Young's senior finals, in spring 1979, he received word that his father had suffered a debilitating stroke, prompting him to drop out of school and move back to Long Island.

Still consumed with the politics of Central America, Young began volunteering, teaching refugees to read in a classroom at the local Methodist church. After finishing undergrad and law school, he went on to work for the Central American Refugee Center, eventually becoming one of the region's leading advocates on behalf of its growing Latino population.

For months, Young and some of his colleagues had been especially troubled. At town meetings and in the online comments of local news coverage, residents voiced alarm that the Ecuadorians would bring with them the very gang violence that they were fleeing. The fears weren't based in reality—Suffolk County had just recorded its safest year on record—but they were real nonetheless. They were the same fears that have driven centuries of hostility toward arriving immigrant populations.

"There was a really poisoned environment," Young recalled. "A traffic cam caught you? Blame it on illegal immigration. If taxes went up, and when there was a cutback in the football program, folks from the school said, 'It's because we're spending X amount of additional dollars on English-as-a-second-language programs.' Whatever's bad in your life, you blame the illegals."

The hostility was often expressed explicitly. "A white woman came up to me and says, 'You make my skin crawl,'" Young said, recalling a confrontation that took place at the Catholic church he attended in nearby Farmingville. "'Why are you with them instead of your own?'"

It wasn't the first time Young had heard some form of that question: Why was he working on behalf of *those people*? And each time elicited the memory of being twelve years old and riding the local bus with his mother. An immigrant worker couldn't figure out how to pay his fare—he had the money; he just didn't know how to deposit it in the collection box. The line of people behind him, waiting to board, grew restless, as did many of the passengers. When she realized what was going on, Young's mother sprung from her seat, pulled several coins from her pocket, and paid the man's fare.

"Everyone will tell you stories about how great their immigrant ancestors were," she told Pat after having returned to her seat. "But nobody wants to help immigrants today."

In recent years, the five- or six-mile stretch where day laborers gathered each morning had been transformed into a corridor of hate. White locals would shout taunts out their car windows at the waiting workers. The immigrants who came to Young's refugee center each day had friends and family members who'd reported being attacked. The consensus was that local police either didn't care or couldn't be trusted not to use the occasion of an immigrant's reporting that he or she had been harmed as an opening to inquire about the victim's citizenship status.

The days and weeks following a racially motivated hate attack often involve public performances of shock—How could this happen? And how could it happen here?—particularly from those eager to believe that their hometown or community is incapable of harboring the kind of racial hatred that can turn homicidal. Young knew better.

7

BRIAN HARMON HAD FIRST MET the Conroys that spring when he moved his family to Medford. Having grown up in this part of Long Island, Harmon knew how important youth sports were to the local culture, and that his son's and daughter's experience at the local schools could be defined by the connections they made on the athletic fields. And so, one of Harmon's first calls after arriving was to Bob Conroy, a power player in local youth athletics.

Conroy was a larger-than-life figure, boisterous and self-assured, who within moments had rolled out a red carpet for the neighborhood's new family. He escorted Harmon and his eight-year-old son through the equipment room, showing him where the local teams stored their gear. When Harmon mentioned that his daughter, then twelve, had a rough day at softball practice, Conroy suggested she try lacrosse and ultimately gifted the girl a lacrosse stick that had belonged to his own daughter.

Conroy enlisted Harmon to join him as a coach on one of the fourth-grade football teams that fall. Conroy and his assistants were a self-serious bunch, chain-smoking cigarettes on the sidelines as they shouted at their young players, stressing the importance of athletic success above all else. Soon Harmon began seeing himself as a bit of a counterweight, providing the players with a sense of sanity and perspective. While Conroy extolled the virtues of helmet-cracking tackles, Harmon tried to instill strategy fundamentals. Where Conroy was harsh, Harmon sought to be understanding.

Yet, despite their differences in style and temperament, Harmon liked Conroy, and admired the role he played as a booster for their small community. Which is why, when he sat down with a cup of coffee and a copy of *Newsday* on the morning of November 10, 2008, Harmon was stunned by what he saw on the front page.

They had been dubbed the "Patchogue Seven": seven local high school boys who together had been charged with the hate crime killing of Marcelo Lucero. According to the media coverage at the time, their ringleader, and the boy alleged to have stabbed Lucero, was seventeen-year-old Jeff Conroy—Bob Conroy's oldest son. Harmon was mortified. What kind of place was this where he had just moved his kids? "Beaner hopping"? What kind of community was this?

But, before long, his mind turned to the Conroy family. For years, Harmon had worked as a reporter and editor at the *New York Daily News*, often covering the types of high-profile murder cases that the Lucero killing was sure to become. Nothing about his interactions with Bob had led him to believe the small-town athletic booster was capable of handling the crush of media that Harmon knew would soon land atop him. And so, he put on a shirt and tie and drove to the county courthouse.

As the crowds awaited Jeff Conroy's arraignment, Harmon was able to squeeze his way into the row behind the boy's father and whisper instructions into his ear. "Don't say anything to the press," Harmon implored. "Walk straight out and to your car. Keep as plain of a look as possible. Don't come across as angry. But also, don't smile." Harmon walked a few paces behind as Bob Conroy, moments after his son was charged with murder, did his best to follow those instructions. When they got back to the Conroy home, Harmon offered to serve as family spokesman through the course of the trial. But then he found out about the tattoo.

On his jail intake form, Jeff Conroy had disclosed that he had a swastika tattooed on his leg.

"Inmate Conroy, Jeffrey #597901 is a self-admitted White Supremacist," the officer who processed him recorded on the form. "During an interview on 11/10/08, inmate Conroy stated that he doesn't consider himself a White Supremacist, but he did say that he does have racist thoughts and beliefs. He stated that he was raised in a home where his parents held racist beliefs. Conroy further added that he has never been a member of any White Supremacist organization, but he does follow White Supremacist activities on the Internet. Inmate Conroy has a tattoo of a swastika on his leg."

During Conroy's trial, his childhood best friend would testify to giving Conroy that tattoo and another earlier that year. The two had been watching the HBO prison drama *Oz* and decided it would be cool to give each other prison tattoos. They looked up the steps online and bought ink from a local Michaels crafts store. The first symbol that Conroy wanted was a single lightning bolt—which to the untrained eye resembles the Gatorade logo but doubles as a key part of Nazi iconography. Conroy would later tell another friend that it was meant to symbolize "white power." A few weeks later, the boys met up again for more ink. This time, Conroy said, he wanted his friend to tattoo a swastika on his thigh, quipping that "If I ever go to jail, I'm screwed."

Harmon was sitting in his basement home office a few days later, scrolling through Jeff Conroy's Myspace page when he saw a post about the small, improvised tattoo. He ran to the phone and dialed Bob Conroy. "Yeah, I know," the accused boy's father told him, adding that it was just a stupid mistake by a stupid teen. No deeper meaning, he assured Brian.

"This is not right," Harmon told him in reply, timbre in his voice. "I'm no longer comfortable speaking on your behalf."

• • •

We don't know the precise extent of Jeff Conroy's exposure to white supremacist ideology—he later denied his initial statements to police, and law enforcement officials told me that they did not probe further his online activities for signs of radicalization. But we do know that if he was frequenting white supremacist websites, he had likely encountered a torrent of anti-immigrant rhetoric.

American racial politics are often taught in a black-white paradigm, obscuring the complexities of the country's ethnic demographics while also presenting an overly simplistic understanding of white supremacists. To the extent that many of us understand American white supremacists, it's often through the images of hooded Klan riders carrying out acts of violence against black Americans. But the American definition of whiteness has expanded and contracted over time. The enemies of the white supremacist are not just those who appear dark skinned, but rather anyone whose presence and procreation threatens a society predicated upon Anglo-protestant dominance.

The Ku Klux Klan, one of the world's oldest terrorist organizations, was founded in Pulaski, Tennessee, in December 1865, conceived in the American Whitelash that followed the Civil War, "when time was out of joint in the South and the social order was battered and turned upside down," historian David Chalmers writes in *Hooded Americanism: The First Century of the Ku Klux Klan*, a definitive history of the organization's first hundred years.

It began with six former officers in the Confederate army, who donned disguises and went for nighttime rides. Within a handful of years, however, the Klan had spread in both scope and mission. "As a secret, nocturnal organization operating during lawless times," Chalmers writes, "the Klan soon turned into a vigilante force. To restore order meant returning the Negro to the field—just as long as he didn't do too well there—and the prewar leaders to their former seats of power. And so the masked Klansmen rode out across the land."

This initial Klan spread across the South, serving as the enforcers of the pre–Civil War racial order and the front line in the resistance against Reconstruction-era attempts to build a multiracial democracy. Targets included black politicians and militias, the Radical Republicans who supported black suffrage, and black schoolteachers. "In practically every one of the states in which the Klan rode, it sprang or expanded into active life with the advent of the new Radical governments of 1867 and 1868," Chalmers writes. "In all cases, the dates of the Klan explosion corresponded to either the establishment of the new Radical governments or the failure of these democratic efforts at biracial political harmony."

This initial iteration of the Klan ultimately petered out by 1871, due in part to its own successes and the success of the Southern backlash to Reconstruction more broadly. But the Klan was reborn in the early twentieth century, sparked by a number of overlapping factors, starting with the original organization's lionization in D. W. Griffith's 1915 silent film *The Birth of a Nation*, which depicted the hooded knights as brave defenders of white women from emancipated slaves. The three-hour-long epic reached a large audience and was the first motion picture ever screened at the White House, by President Woodrow Wilson. Two other contributing factors were the lynching in Atlanta of a Jewish businessman named Leo Frank, who had been falsely accused of rape and murder, and the resulting media spectacle; and automobile magnate Henry Ford's promoting anti-Semitic propaganda in the newspaper he'd purchased: the *Dearborn Independent*. Ninety-two consecutive issues carried a series of articles claiming that a vast Jewish conspiracy was tainting the United States. The man who introduced assembly line mass production to the world then compiled the pieces into a four-volume set of booklets titled *The International Jew: The World's Foremost Problem*, distributing a half million copies at home and abroad.

Inspired by Griffith's film and Frank's lynching, an Atlanta preacher named William Joseph Simmons began researching the original Klan and resolved to relaunch his own version. He ultimately joined forces with Mary Elizabeth Tyler and Edward Young Clarke, who ran the Southern Publicity Association, a fundraising, public relations, and marketing agency. (Clarke's father, a former Confederate colonel, owned the *Atlanta Constitution*.) They saw this new Klan as a potential cash cow with mass appeal to white Americans but believed—at a time when there were still relatively few black Americans living outside of the Southeast—that the group's mission would need to expand beyond just bigotry toward black people and insisting on the pre–Civil War racial order. If the aim of the original Klan was the economic subjugation and political disenfranchisement of the newly emancipated black Americans, the second Klan was even more ambitious and expansive in its objectives.

This new Klan seized on the anxiety that, for many Americans, had accompanied the rapid societal changes of the 1920s: urbanization had given rise to bustling cities and the cultural explosion of the Jazz Age, and new waves of immigrants had brought with them a "Red Scare" about the influence of Communism. Furthermore, gender roles were fundamentally changing: women had gained the right to vote with the passage of the Nineteenth Amendment, the flapper subculture had challenged sexual and gender norms, and new advancements in birth control meant women were having more sex and fewer children. The best way to market the Klan, its new leaders knew, was to play to the sense among many white Americans that traditional American values were under attack by cosmopolitan enemies.

According to historian Linda Gordon, author of *The Second Coming of the KKK: The Ku Klux Klan of the 1920s and the American Political Tradition*, "These were not only black people but also Jews, Catholics, and immigrants, the big-city dwellers who were tempting Americans with immoral pleasures—sex, alcohol, and music." The hate group's revival, she writes, "took off by melding racism and ethnic bigotry with evangelical Protestant morality."

This Klan became perhaps the most powerful social and political force in American life—stronger in states across the North and Midwest, Gordon notes, where the cultural and sociological fights of integration and urbanization were playing out more rapidly, than it was in the South—at times holding its own political primaries in local elections and, in 1925, marching more than thirty thousand people down Pennsylvania Avenue in the nation's capital as part of a weekend of public events meant as a show of the organization's strength. "Phantom-like hosts of the Ku Klux Klan spread their white robe over the most historic thoroughfare yesterday in one of the greatest demonstrations this city has ever known," the *Washington Post* reported the next morning.

The ideological pillars of the second Klan, the doctrinal forebear of today's white supremacist movement, were racism, nativism, fraternalism, Christian evangelicalism, and populism. Its members bonded over a shared skepticism of immigrants, Catholics, Jews, Communists, feminists, and, later, President Franklin D. Roosevelt's New Deal.

"The Klan built a politics of resentment, reflecting but also fomenting antipathy toward those who it defined as threatening Americanism," Gordon writes. "By blaming immigrants and non-Protestants for stealing jobs and government from 'true' Americans, it stayed away from criticism of those who wielded economic power. Instead it blamed 'elites,' typically presented as big-city liberal professionals, secular urbanites who promoted cosmopolitanism (and were thus insufficiently patriotic) and looked down on Klanspeople as stupid and/or irrational and/or out of step with modernity. This disrespect for the Klan only intensified its hostility and sense of righteousness."

The reconfigured KKK was largely defunct by the end of the 1920s, after its leadership was engulfed in a series of scandals, but its rapid rise to power underscores the appeal of fundamentalist populist movements in moments of whitelash to cultural, societal, and political upheaval. "The Klan spread, strengthened, and radicalized preexisting nativist and racist sentiments among the white population," Gordon writes. The Klan argued not just for an end to non-"Nordic" immigration but also for deporting such immigrants who were already living here. And it could claim as a chief accomplishment its role in helping Congress's enthusiastic passage of the 1924 Immigration Act, which assigned ethnic quotas and limited the total annual number of immigrants permitted into the United States. The new law, also called the Johnson-Reed Act, had been cosponsored by Albert Johnson, a Washington congressman—and proud Klansman.

"Congress was deluged with letters registering grave fears at the prospect that the 'distinct American type,' undergirded by the northern and Western European 'Nordic race,' might be swamped," notes historian David R. Roediger. "Ku Klux Klan membership swelled as Klan leaders promised 'real whites' that the organization would defend the victimized 'American race'. . . 'a blend of various peoples of the so-called Nordic race' against the 'mongrelized.'"

Xenophobic bigotries remained a chief animating factor of the white supremacist iterations to follow during the next one hundred years. The violence of the skinhead movement of the 1970s in the United Kingdom—initially a multiracial, working-class coalition—began with attacks by white Londoners against Pakistani immigrants. When it later crossed the Atlantic, the skinheads found fertile recruitment ground in Southern California, where white residents were among the first to experience significant levels of Central and South American immigration. The neo-Nazi movement preaches about a Jewish conspiracy to undermine the white populace by introducing migrant blood—essentially, they argue that Hitler was right. The need to "save" the white race from colored outsiders has been a chief ideological underpinning of a century of American racists. In 1977, Klansmen Tom Metzger and David Duke, pivotal figures in the movement's recent history, organized a "border watch" along the southern border. (While Duke promised hundreds of Klansmen were participating, it ultimately amounted to more of a publicity stunt than actual border patrol, with just a handful of people taking part.) Their offspring, today's white supremacists, are likewise mobilized by concerns about an influx of migrants and refugees—the so-called great replacement of the country's white population, a racist conspiracy theory popularized by the 1973 French dystopian novel *The Camp of the Saints*, which in recent decades has joined *The Turner Diaries* in the white supremacist canon.

Similar to their forefathers, modern white supremacists seek to influence national politics, often by laundering their bigoted beliefs into mainstream political consciousness through sympathetic commentators and politicians and with the help of agenda-driven think tanks. Like the officials in New Orleans, who released a fraudulent list of Italian murderers, these think tanks often utilize bent and skewed statistics to portray Latino immigrants as uniquely violent, carriers of disease, and a net negative for the economy.

"A lot of the racist Right looking for a way to express themselves found immigration a big opening," Frank Sharry, the immigrant rights activist, told me.

"There is no question, there is a clear through line from the white supremacists who are xenophobes in three-piece suits making their policy arguments and [violence]," Sharry added.

PROSECUTOR MEGAN O'DONNELL HADN'T SEEN a case quite like the Patchogue Seven in her decade with the Suffolk County prosecutor's office. In recent years, the office had handled hate crimes in which day laborers had been harassed or targeted. But this was the first murder of its kind to cross her desk.

"I don't think anyone, including myself, could understand how or why this could happen," O'Donnell told me. "I'm white . . . many of my friends are Latino and dark skinned. I guess it was something that I was constantly picturing: my friends—my colleague that I worked with, or one of my good friends—it could have so easily been them. It could have easily touched my life [directly]."

All seven boys had been charged, and what shocked law enforcement the most was that it was clear this had not been their first time out beaner hopping. Here, in one of New York's nicest suburban enclaves, clean-cut high school athletes had been committing hate crime sprees.

O'Donnell set aside the question on everyone's minds: Was Jeff Conroy really a white supremacist or perhaps just a troubled teen who'd made a dumb decision? The way she saw it, her job wasn't to litigate his inner self or mind-set, just to get him convicted of his crime. "He was not walking out of that courtroom as a free person. It was really between the manslaughter and the murder [charges]," she told me of her strategy going into trial, noting one key piece of evidence: medical experts had concluded that Conroy had twisted the knife after he'd plunged it into Lucero. "I knew that was going to come down to that minute type of detail, an intent to kill or not.

"We had very good evidence. The investigator that night got statements from all of the young men; we had the bloody knife; Lucero's friend was an eyewitness—a lot of things that sometimes victims don't have," she explained. "We could never prove what was in Conroy's head."

But soon O'Donnell was confronted with an obstacle she had not expected: finding a willing and unbiased jury.

In a typical felony case, it would take about a week and a half to find twelve jurors acceptable to both the prosecution and the defense. But jury selection in the Conroy case dragged on twice as long. While the pool of potential jurors typically includes about 150 people, this case cycled through close to 450 jurors. The reason was not, O'Donnell said, because the people they had brought in were looking for a way to get out of jury duty. Instead, many of them were acknowledging that they felt too strongly about illegal immigration to administer justice, especially with a defendant so young. "It was certainly not that those people were saying, 'I don't feel sympathy for the victim. [It was] I really don't think I can be fair to the prosecution; I really just have strong opinions against illegal immigration.'" Asked if they could be objective about an immigrant—even one who had been murdered—most of the Suffolk County residents who were asked told the court that, honestly, they could not.

But they eventually found a jury, and on March 18, 2010, the hate crime murder trial *People of the State of New York v. Jeffrey Conroy* began.

In her opening statement, Assistant District Attorney O'Donnell set the scene: "On November 8, 2008, the hunt was on. Seven teenagers, one of which was the defendant, Jeffrey Conroy, wilding, roaming the streets of Patchogue for one purpose and one purpose only: to find a Hispanic person to randomly and physically attack. The defendant and his friends were not in Patchogue looking to meet up with other friends, they were not in Patchogue looking to go to a party. They were in Patchogue for one reason and one reason only: looking for blood, specifically Mexican blood, a sport that the defendant callously called 'Mexican-hopping.' That was the plan for the night . . . this plan, as well as each and every choice that the defendant made and each and every action that the defendant took, caused the death of Marcelo Lucero."

Over the course of the trial, prosecutors would argue that the killing was not a sudden crime committed in a moment of rage but rather the result of a deliberate plan. Conroy and his friends, they argued, had done precisely what they had set out to do that night.

Conroy's defense was one often employed by those accused of prejudice. He argued, in essence, that the fact that he had black and brown friends made it impossible for him to have acted out of racial malice. The trial became a tug-of-war between two Jeff Conroys: the well-liked high school athlete with a Hispanic ex-girlfriend and the young punk with a swastika tattoo who set out that night on a mission of hate.

Friends of the family told the *New York Times* that Jeffrey Conroy was "warm and patient with younger boys, admired by peers and adults as a promising athlete, and friendly with people of many ethnicities." Chief among the defenses offered by his supporters was the fact that Conroy had a half sister who was part Puerto Rican, and his longtime on-again, off-again girlfriend was Bolivian. In his opening statement, Conroy's defense attorney noted that the two dozen or so supporters in the room were of various ethnicities. "He had friends of every race, creed, and color, and they've all been in his house when I was there, so I've seen it," stated Marc Negrin, a close friend of the Conroy family. "All these things we're hearing and we're reading is not the young man that I know."

Defense attorney William Keahon told the jurors, "He comes from a family with four other brothers and sisters, plus his step-sister. Lives in Medford. The mother teaches Sunday school at a born-again church, and she taught there for either five or seven years and was in charge of the Sunday school program, teaching Christian values. That's the family he came from.

"Now, can a good athlete be involved in this stuff? Sure, they can. But a kid that's in those sports—and he's very, very good at them—is this really a kid that's going to go out and try to, with others, beat up one other person or two people?"

Even though police found the murder weapon in his pocket, and, later that night, he signed a five-page confession, Jeff Conroy insisted in the courtroom that he had not, in fact, stabbed Lucero. It was another teen, Conroy now claimed, but he had lied to the cops in order to protect his friend. "I didn't know that the guy was hurt bad. He told me—he promised that the guy wasn't hurt," Conroy testified. Furthermore, the tattoos were not meant to be white supremacist symbols; they were just a joke.

Keahon, in his closing statement, spoke directly to the jury members: "Those of you that believe that he stabbed him; you know this is not intentional murder. You know it's not even manslaughter in the first degree. You know it's not even that he intended to cause serious physical injury. When you intend to kill somebody, if you don't do it with the first stab and the way that went in, is it fair to assume . . . that there would be multiple stab wounds?"

The jury deliberated for four days before returning their verdict: guilty of hate crime manslaughter and gang assault. Later, members would tell reporters that they did not buy Conroy's claims of innocence, but they were not convinced that he had intended to kill Lucero. "The hunting season is over," Joselo Lucero told reporters outside of the courtroom. "At least for now."

Yet the Lucero murder and Conroy conviction underscore another reality of hatred in America and white America's difficulties grappling with it: even the teenager who tattoos a swastika on himself, murders an immigrant, and is convicted of a hate crime insists he is not a racist. Then what *is* a racist, if not someone who commits a violent act of racism?

"I'm nothing like what the papers said about me," Conroy said adamantly in a jailhouse interview with the *Times* after his conviction. "I'm not a white supremacist or anything like that. I'm not this serious racist kid everyone thinks I am."

9

WHEN I CAN, I LIKE to read contemporaneous accounts of the country's racial history: magazine accounts of race riots, newspaper dispatches from lynchings. Often, I find, there is as much to be learned from how history was recorded and framed as there is from the basic facts of what happened. But of all the old periodicals I've come across in bookstores and vintage shops, a copy of the April 9, 1968, edition of the now-defunct *Chicago Daily News* is the one that, in recent years, I've found myself revisiting most often.

It was a special twelve-page edition of the afternoon paper, published five days after the assassination of Martin Luther King Jr. in Memphis. The now-faded newspaper features original reporting about the fallout that followed his murder, reactions from Chicago luminaries, and a eulogy written by poet Gwendolyn Brooks, who, eighteen years earlier, had become the first black American to win a Pulitzer Prize. "His word still burns the center of the sun, above the thousands and the hundred thousands," Brooks wrote. "The word was Justice. It was spoken. So it shall be spoken. So it shall be done."

Yet, from the first time I opened the torn pages, my eyes have found themselves drawn to the second to last, which, amid an issue dedicated largely to exalting a slain American saint, features a column from Mike Royko.

Royko, thirty-five at the time, was at the front end of a three-decade career that made him a household name in Chicago and perhaps the city's most recognizable journalist. He'd become a columnist four years before King's assassination and would win a Pulitzer of his own four years after it. Given the somber tone of the preceding pages, I expected a writerly yarn with soaring prose about King's mission and morality. Instead, Royko delivered a sweeping societal indictment.

"FBI agents are looking for the man who pulled the trigger, and surely they will find him," he begins. "But it doesn't matter if they do or they don't. They can't catch everybody, and Martin Luther King was executed by a firing squad that numbered in the millions. They took part, from all over the country, pouring words of hate into the ear of the assassins. The man with the gun did what he was told. Millions of bigots, subtle and obvious, put it in his hand and assured him he was doing the right thing."

Royko doesn't let up from there, going on for hundreds of words, laying the blame not just on the avid racists but also on those who peddle division with rhetorical sleight of hand. The prose is unsparing. The culpability is widely assigned: The southern redneck. The northern disc jockey. The cowardly white mayors. "The Eastern and Southern European immigrant or his kid who seems to be convinced that in 40 or 50 years he built this country. . . . They all took their place in King's firing squad. And behind them were the subtle ones, those who never say anything bad but just nod when the bigot throws out his strong opinions."

This piece—and, really, it should be read in its entirety—kept coming to mind as I considered the debate that took place in Patchogue and across Suffolk County after the murder of Marcelo Lucero. It's the kind of rhetoric that has been a mainstay of the public discourse accompanying the rise in racial violence since Barack Obama's election in 2008. Nearly everyone condemns racial violence unequivocally, but few seem to agree on a thornier question: To what extent is the gun in the hand of those who stoked the hatred as much as it is he who pulled the trigger?

• • •

In the years that have followed the 2016 presidential election, it has been a parlor game among prognosticators to identify which previous political figure foretold the eventual rise of Donald Trump.

There was the election of Rudy Giuliani as mayor of New York, after he ran a brash 1993 campaign that stoked the city's racial division and kissed up to the city's brutal police force in order to dethrone David Dinkins, New York's first black mayor. At one point, Giuliani helped incite a riot of white police officers at city hall. "The cops held up several of the most crude drawings of Dinkins, black, performing perverted sex acts," wrote legendary columnist Jimmy Breslin in *Newsday*. "And then, here was one of them calling across the top of his beer can held to his mouth," referring to Dinkins as "a nigger mayor."

There was Joe Arpaio, the longtime sheriff of Maricopa County, Arizona, whose entire public reputation and platform was his inhumane treatment of immigrants. And, of course, there was Sarah Palin, the Republicans' 2008 vice presidential candidate who became a conservative media celebrity largely because of her appeal to the populist, conspiratorial fringe of the GOP base, her willingness to scapegoat the mainstream media, and her aversion to factual accuracy.

Even so, I've become increasingly convinced that no political career more portended what was to come than the rise of Suffolk County Executive Steve Levy.

Levy was a middle-class kid, born in Brooklyn and raised for ten years in Queens before his family moved out to Holbrook, a Long Island community about fifty miles from Manhattan. He stayed local for college, at Stony Brook University, and law school, at St. John's University, before leaping into politics. Back then, Levy considered himself a pro–civil rights, pro–government Democrat.

Both of his parents had been, so what else would he be? "Typical young idealist who wanted to change the world," Levy says of himself back then. In 1985, at just twenty-five years old, he put his name on the ballot for an open seat in the Suffolk County Legislature.

"I had no backing from the party or any kind of rich benefactors or corporate entities. I just started knocking on doors from April through November and eked out an election I wasn't supposed to win," he told me. "I was a Democrat running in the most heavily Republican district in Suffolk County, and there's eighteen districts there. And I won just by being nonpartisan. 'What do you need? Is there a problem in your neighborhoods?' I was always pretty independent minded."

Before long, Levy had become one of the most popular elected officials on Long Island. He made property taxes one of his early signature issues—residents of Suffolk County paid some of the highest taxes in the country—taking fiscal positions at times more conservative than his Republican colleagues but earning the support of an electorate made up of relatively moderate white Democrats. In 2000 he ran and was elected to the state legislature, and then in 2003 he mounted a campaign to become the Suffolk County executive. His Democratic primary opponent attacked him from the left, noting that Levy had opposed a government-funded hiring program that helped undocumented immigrants find work. "I won by a two-to-one margin," Levy recalled. He then easily won the general election and took office in 2004.

"We were seeing, because of the heated economy in the nineties, a magnet for an influx of people from Central and South America to help in construction and other parts of the economy," Levy said. "And both sides of the aisle looked the other way. The Democrats loved it because it was potential new voters, and the Republicans loved it because it was giving them cheap labor. And in the meantime, you have the average resident saying '*What* is going on here?'" Before long, immigration had become one of Levy's leading issues.

Long Islanders' concerns, he insisted, were reasonable. Many of them had moved there to chase what they considered the American dream: backyard swimming pools and school districts with a handbook full of extracurriculars. Now it was routine to see day laborers standing along city streets and cramming into apartments by the dozen in order to save on rent. It's not xenophobic, Levy insisted to me, to be uncomfortable with that shift.

"So many of them were unfortunately painted with this brush of being bigoted," he observed. "Everyone was being painted with the same brush"—whether it was a mother concerned about a crowded apartment of day laborers next door or "a guy with a swastika on his leg attacking people."

By the time Marcelo Lucero was killed, Levy was considered the primary opponent of local immigrants' rights groups, who believed (he insists unfairly) that his rhetoric and policies had turned the local population against the arriving migrant workers—thereby putting their lives in danger. He doubled down on strict zoning laws to get rid of overcrowded workers' residences and proposed that police officers double as immigration agents in order to round up undocumented residents.

He was "particularly dangerous to the immigrant community," Pat Young, who has since founded Hofstra Law School's Immigration Law Clinic, told me, in part because as an elected Democrat, his words and stances could radicalize voters who would typically tune out anti-immigrant Republicans. "He scared me," added national activist Frank Sharry of America's Voice. "He looked like he had figured out the Democratic lunch-pail lane with a heavy dollop of racism." Even Bob Conroy, before his death, began publicly blaming Levy for radicalizing his son. The argument goes that by suggesting that the arrival of immigrants was a crisis threatening local residents' safety and security, Levy and other elected officials had, in essence, deputized vigilantes such as Conroy to respond to that threat.

"If you put a picture of me before this kid, he wouldn't know who I was," Levy told me in response. "The father didn't want to take ownership of the fact that the son became a racist, so he was looking to blame other people." There is no connection, he still insists, between Long Island's very public fear of new immigrants and the killing of Marcelo Lucero.

"One of the points that I made at the time is that hate crimes happen anywhere," Levy told me the first time we connected by phone. "What happened in this case is there was far more focus on it because many tried to inaccurately tie it to the illegal immigration debate that was stewing at the time."

The immigration politics and rhetoric of the mid-2000s would resurface a decade later, as an American presidential candidate launched his populist campaign for office by warning that the migrants crossing the southern border from Mexico were "rapists." From there, Donald Trump went on to trot out families of Americans killed by crimes committed by immigrants and making the construction of a giant wall on the southern border the central (ultimately broken) promise of his eventual administration. "Trump was very, very good about coming up with an allegory," Jim Sensenbrenner, the former Republican congressman from Wisconsin, told me. "'Build the wall and make the Mexicans pay for it'—and all of us can understand what the wall is."

In that sense, the murder of Marcelo Lucero was a warning of what the decade to come would bring. Recurrent in the years after his death would be acts of anti-immigrant violence that were immediately followed by debate about to what extent these acts had been spurred on by intolerant, overheated, and explicitly racist political rhetoric coming from political commentators, elected officials, and the White House.

Donald J. Trump launched his presidential campaign in June 2015 by declaring to the supporters and press gathered at Trump Tower in Manhattan: "When Mexico sends its people, they're not sending their best." Two months later, two white Boston men beat and urinated on a homeless Latino man, with one of them telling police later, "Donald Trump was right: all these illegals need to be deported." Two days after Trump's 2016 presidential victory, a twenty-three-year-old white man in High Springs, Florida, struck an unsuspecting Hispanic man in the back of the head, proclaiming, "This is for Donald Trump!"

The forty-fifth president of the United States spent significant portions of his early years in office specifically targeting immigrants and refugees, stoking fears of caravans of undocumented immigrants storming the southern border and waves of refugees being resettled in suburban America. It was an "invasion," President Trump declared again and again. Then, in August 2019, a twenty-one-year-old white man drove ten hours from suburban Dallas to El Paso, Texas, in order to shoot and kill twenty-two people, specifically targeting Latino immigrants. In an online manifesto, the mass murderer stated explicitly that his own racist views predated Trump's presidency. But he echoed the president's ugly rhetoric about an immigrant invasion and cited the white supremacist replacement theory.

In 2010 Steve Levy switched parties, registering as a Republican. Nevertheless, he said he deplores Donald Trump's repeated targeting of migrants from Central and South America.

"You know, when the president uses inartful language that can be misinterpreted that he's saying Mexicans are rapists, that's going too far," he told me. "'We're going to ban all Muslims'—that's stupid." Levy did not vote for Trump in 2016, due in large part to the candidate's incendiary speech. "There are cases where Trump goes too far with his rhetoric."

In each instance, Trump's advisers and defenders would argue that it was unfair to place the blame for the deranged actions of others on him, no matter his language. Yet time and time again, experts on extremism and hate speech would stress that degrading and demonizing language toward specific ethnic and racial groups by powerful political leaders can bring about predictable outcomes.

In the wake of the El Paso shootings, Nathan P. Kalmoe, an assistant professor at Louisiana State University who studies hate speech, told the *New York Times:* "The people who carry out these attacks are already violent and hateful people. But top political leaders and partisan media figures encourage extremism when they endorse white supremacist ideas and play with violent language. Having the most powerful person on Earth echo their hateful views may even give extremists a sense of impunity."

Some consider Steve Levy the villain in the story of Marcelo Lucero's death. "Conroy may have plunged the knife into Lucero's chest," Mirta Ojito writes. "But the culprit, it was almost universally believed, was Steve Levy." He was, after all, the most powerful local voice decrying illegal immigration and heightening public concerns about tax money being spent on behalf of Long Island's undocumented aliens. What I wanted to know from Levy was how, if at all, the passage of time had either shifted or hardened his position. By the time we first spoke, more than a decade had passed since the murder, and perhaps hindsight had been accompanied by reconsideration.

Much had changed. Levy was no longer in office, having opted against running for a third term. And, of course, he was no longer a Democrat. He'd changed political parties, he told me, because, in his view, the Democratic Party had become too "obsessed with racial identity politics." Levy published a book about his time in elected office, titled *Bias in the Media: How the Media Switched Against Me After I Switched Parties.* In another change, Levy voted for Donald Trump in 2020.

During our first call, Levy told me that it was clear from a law enforcement perspective that white supremacist groups had not been taken seriously enough. He, like many white Americans, sees violent white supremacy as a dwindling force. There are multitudes fewer Klansmen today than a century ago, he'd noted. Yet it's clear that their ability to spread their message is simpler than ever.

"We've always had these haters, we've always had the hate crimes, but now we have social media and the Internet. . . . We've got fewer white supremacists with a greater means to do bad stuff," he observed. "You have some grand wizard in Minnesota who can send out instructions to an impressionable kid in Long Island. And something like that can put a disturbed person over the line.

"We spent a great deal of time after 9/11 concentrating on foreign threats and even internal threats to those who fit the profile," he added. "But perhaps we need to give the same type of surveillance and intensity of attention to these white supremacist groups."

Still, Levy told me he had no regrets about his own behavior in the early and mid-2000s. His comments were never, he insisted, anti-immigrant. Even though they could be fiery, he said, the vast majority of people with concerns about illegal immigration are not racists. Maybe 10 percent, he estimated, are "nutcases."

"There's no question that you want to talk truth, but you never want to incite, and there is a balancing act there. I guess it's in the eye of a beholder," Levy reflected. "You can be against illegal immigration and still understand that regardless of whether you're documented or not, you're still a human being who deserves basic human rights. You have to marginalize the idiots."

But how can such white supremacist elements be effectively marginalized when their ideology and rhetoric are mirrored so closely by mainstream political rhetoric? History shows clearly how demonization of immigrants prompts violence toward these new arrivals—and how white supremacist groups have, nearly from their inception, manipulated the fear of immigrants and out-siders to strengthen their ranks. Even if, as Levy suggests, it's just 10 percent of those with political concerns about immigration who are actually capable of violence, that would amount to millions of Americans—and an immigrant's life is imperiled by encountering just a single one of them. If we are to be a nation and society that hold both multiracial democracy and freedom of speech as founda-tional values, what do we do with those who would use one to go to war against the other?

PART III

WHITE RADICALIZATION

When suffering isn't treated with compassion, it seethes and spreads. When fear isn't met with courage, it deceives and disconnects humans from humanity. When ignorance isn't countered with wisdom, it festers and takes root in the hearts of the fearful.

—ARNO MICHAELIS AND PARDEEP SINGH KALEKA,
*The Gift of Our Wounds: A Sikh and a Former
White Supremacist Find Forgiveness After Hate*

10

BY THE TIME HE MADE his final drive, the seven miles from his apartment to the scene of his crime, Wade Michael Page had little left in his life. He'd long been distant from his family, he had almost no money and no career to speak of. He'd always been the type of guy to become despondent after a romantic breakup, and this time had been no different.

The forty-year-old skinhead had moved halfway across the country, from North Carolina to suburban Milwaukee, to be with Misty. They'd met online, first on Facebook and later on the white supremacist message boards they both liked to spend their evenings surfing. She would later tell law enforcement that he'd become increasingly conspiratorial toward the end of their relationship and ultimately broke up with her. It was after that, officials say, that in an act of parting rage, Misty revealed to the Hammerskins, the violent white supremacist skinhead group Page belonged to, that he'd previously dated a woman of color—a mortal sin in the eyes of the movement. They had no choice. They kicked him out.

Page had been a member of the movement for his entire adult life. He'd gone from being a punk rock high school kid in suburban Denver to enlisting in the army and serving at Fort Bragg in North Carolina, where he was exposed to neo-Nazi ideology. But Page's time in the military was short lived: the army discharged him after he showed up to his work assignment drunk. A year or two later, he landed in Southern California as a skinhead rocker, traveling internationally to perform with bands at racist music festivals before ultimately becoming a "patched" member of the Hammerskins.

To study white supremacists is to examine a collection of broken people who see their own hardships and traumas as evidence that they are the world's victims. Their pain and suffering are often real: unaddressed childhood traumas, physical and sexual assaults, economic and educational deprivations. The movement convinces its followers that their failures and flaws are not the result of their choices, or an unlucky spin in the roulette of circumstance, but rather due to a global racial conspiracy far beyond their control. Perhaps most importantly, the movement offers members a family, though one whose loving bonds are forged in shared hatred and delusion.

Yet a security constructed through anger cannot hold. Even the charismatic leader who proclaims through his bullhorn that his frustrations are the fault of "the others" has to return home at sundown to be tormented by his inadequacies. The brokenness that brought these men and women into the movement, that they buried beneath layers of hatred, never left them—it lies in wait for its moment to resurface.

For Page, that moment came in the weeks after his breakup with Misty. He was jobless and alone. The movement that had defined his life and served as a crucial support system was gone. After the Hammerskins threw him out, Page spent the next two months doing little else besides drink, play Xbox, and watch white supremacist videos online. At some point, he began selling off his computers and other belongings. It would have been clear that Page was planning something—had there been anyone still close enough to him to see.

In his 2019 book *Hateland: A Long, Hard Look at America's Extremist Heart*, former Department of Homeland Security official Daryl Johnson outlines the factors that the most radical, violent extremists have in common. After all, there are likely hundreds of thousands if not millions of avowed racists in our country. Yet, by every available count, just a sliver of them carry out acts of violence each year. The violent extremists, he explains, have destabilizing personal factors such as traumatic childhoods, exposure to radicalizing forces such as white supremacist websites and organizations, and the means to actually carry out their violent fantasies. "Extremist ideologies do not themselves cause violence. They do, however, encourage an actor to focus what may otherwise be an incoherent sense of grievance on a specific target," Johnson writes. "They can create a narrative, supplying a sense of purpose and mission to the extremist's actions."

That came to a head for Wade just after ten o'clock on the morning of August 5, 2012, when he guided his red pickup truck down the long driveway that separates the Sikh Temple of Wisconsin, in the small city of Oak Creek, from the main road. Dressed in a white T-shirt and dark pants, he parked, grabbed the 9-millimeter handgun he'd purchased, and found a spot near the entrance, where he'd have a clear shot at anyone who exited the temple.

Page left no manifesto, no explicit guide to decode the aims of his actions that day. But there's futility in searching for clues to questions that have already been answered. "For many, it was unclear in those early hours whether what had happened inside the gurdwara was another tragic incident of gun violence, a hate crime, or both," Deepa Iyer, one of the nation's most prominent South Asian activists, would write later in *We Too Sing America: South Asian, Arab, Muslim, and Sikh Immigrants Shape Our Multiracial Future*. "Those of us working with South Asian, Arab, Muslim, and Sikh immigrant communities had little doubt about the nature of the tragedy."

WHEN I VISITED THE ISLAMIC Center in Cedar Rapids, Iowa, nearly four years later in April 2016, the stream of worshippers began flowing through the door just after twelve thirty in the afternoon. They greeted one another warmly, with hugs and hellos, as they slipped out of their shoes and stripped off their socks. The men, some in suits, others in T-shirts and jeans, filed into the large prayer room on the left, with its white walls and magenta carpet, while the women, many in colorful hijabs, and children continued straight ahead, disappearing into a smaller room of their own.

Hidden here, in the second largest city in the nation's fifth whitest state, is one of the oldest Muslim communities in the nation. As many as 6,000 Muslim families dot the neighborhoods that hug the Cedar River, comprising a small but visible community in a city of 130,000.

The message this morning was delivered from a wooden podium at the front of the prayer room by Hassan Selim, an Egyptian-born imam who had arrived here three years earlier. Despite his commanding authority as a speaker, his boyish looks betray his youth. At the time of my visit, he was just twenty-eight years old and serving as the spiritual leader of the largest of Cedar Rapids's three mosques.

In purposefully protracted prose, Selim explained that it is never justified for a Muslim to slander another person—even if that person is a celebrity or a politician who has attacked Islam.

Heads around the room nodded silently.

He doesn't have to say their names, for the men gathered in front of him and the women listening at the other end of the building all know which politicians he's referencing. "As imams, we have to shed light," Selim would tell me after the prayer service, which eventually grew so full that the lines of congregants overflowed into the hallways; they kneeled prostrate next to the wooden racks that hold the shoes of those in the prayer room. A few feet away sat stacks of pamphlets. *Against Terrorism and Religious Extremism*, read one. *Jihad: Striving for Peace* was the title of another, which declared that the concept of "holy war," often used as a justification for terrorism, has no ideological place in Islam.

"There is so much energy being spent in taking back Islam from the people who have hijacked it," Selim noted with a sigh.

I'd come at a time when American political rhetoric was demonizing Muslims with an intensity rivaling the months that followed 9/11. The Muslims in Cedar Rapids had cringed when then-candidate Donald Trump, shaping up to be the GOP nominee for president, called for a ban on Muslim refugees. And, in the weeks before my visit to Iowa, following an ISIS attack that left thirty-two dead and more than three hundred injured in Brussels, Belgium, they sat horrified as Texas senator Ted Cruz, then Trump's only remaining rival for the Republican nomination, called for police agencies to "patrol and secure Muslim communities before they become radicalized."

In the decade and a half since September 11, 2001, Muslims across the country faced law enforcement scrutiny and monitoring, public suspicion and scorn, and political vilification and the uptick in violence that so often accompanies it. Two days after 9/11, an armed Seattle man set fire to cars parked at the Islamic Idriss

Mosque and then opened fire on worshippers as they exited. That same day, a man poured gasoline on a Pakistani American restaurant in Salt Lake City in an attempt to burn it to the ground. In September 2004 a man threw a Molotov cocktail at the Islamic Center in El Paso, barely missing children playing nearby. Two years later, an Illinois man pleaded guilty in federal court after blowing up the van of a Palestinian American family. In 2008 three Tennessee men spray-painted swastikas and the words "white power" on a mosque in Columbia.

While there had been 28 reported crimes against Muslims in 2000, there were 481 of them in 2001. Each year for the next decade, that number remained above 100. Those tallies, of course, are likely significant undercounts.

Now, after a decade and a half of laboring to assure the country that theirs was a religion of peace—that the average American Muslim was as different from Jihadi terrorists as the average American Christian was from murderous Klansmen—the Muslims I spoke to in Cedar Rapids feared a new round of political rhetoric, sparked by the horrors committed by ISIS, would erase years of work toward convincing their neighbors that they belonged. "When this talk of surveillance kicks up, our people start to get nervous," Selim told me. "If policing is ever done here the way Mr. Cruz spoke about it, it would be absolutely destructive to the relationship the Muslims here have with this city."

And the vitriol and violence had not been limited just to Muslims but also to others who were mistakenly perceived as Muslim. Just four days after the 9/11 attacks, forty-two-year-old Frank Roque prowled the streets of Mesa, Arizona, having told a waiter at Applebee's that he was going to "go out and shoot some towelheads" as retaliation for the terrorist attacks.

Balbir Singh Sodhi was planting flowers outside of Mesa Star, the gas station he had opened only a year before, when Roque found him and shot him five times in the back. "I am a patriot!" he declared when the police arrested him the following day. Yet his victim, Sodhi, was not a Muslim, he was a Sikh.

Sikhism, founded in the fifteenth century in Punjab, the South Asian region currently divided between India and Pakistan, is a monotheistic doctrine that among its core tenets emphasizes treating others equally and living truthfully. Today there are tens of millions of Sikhs worldwide, including more than a million in the United States.

Because their men grow long beards and wear colorful turbans, Sikhs have often come under attack by those who mistake them for Muslims. Sikh activist groups have documented hundreds of attacks in the decades since 9/11, none more deadly than the one in Oak Creek.

WITHIN A FEW MINUTES OF Wade Michael Page's arrival, a forty-one-year-old priest named Sita Singh had pulled into the parking lot to relieve his older brother Ranjit, forty-nine, who'd been on temple duty that morning. The older brother had been in America for nearly sixteen years, having left his family back in India in search of a more prosperous life in the States. The younger brother had followed just a year earlier, first living in New York before joining his brother in Wisconsin. Both spent much of their time volunteering at the gurdwara.

As the brothers talked near the temple doors, Page got out of his truck and walked toward them. The approaching stranger caught the eye of the Singh brothers, whose friends believe they were likely eager to greet the unfamiliar face. Page raised his weapon and pulled the trigger, striking both men. Two Sikh children who were playing nearby ran inside to warn the worshippers. "Someone killed the *babaji*!" they screamed, according to a full account of the shooting later provided by Pardeep Singh Kaleka, the son of the temple's chief priest.

The scene was chaotic, with people running in every direction to find cover and desperately calling both the police and their loved ones. Eighteen-year-old Harpreet Saini was home when he got a frantic call from his aunt. "Where's your mom? Did she go to the church? Call her to make sure she's okay!" His mother had tried and failed to wake both Harpreet and his older brother, Kamal, to join her at the temple that morning. The family had come to America from India in 2004 and moved to the Oak Creek region just a few years before the attack. His mother soon became a regular, never missing a service. Her family would tease her that the temple was her second home. Harpreet began desperately calling her phone as Kamal raced to the temple, but his mother would not pick up. He began to pray.

Page worked his way randomly through the temple, firing upon anyone he encountered. A group of women had been in the kitchen, preparing roti and other food for lunch after the service when they heard the gunfire. They dashed for cover, at least fifteen of them cowering on the floor of the kitchen pantry. According to some accounts of that day, Harpreet's mother, forty-one-year-old Paramjit Kaur, instead ran to the temple, to pray for God's protection. She was still there, on her knees, when Page found her and pulled the trigger. Page encountered eighty-four-year-old Suveg Singh Khattra outside of the library and shot him in the head. Next, he forced his way into the living quarters, where Punjab Singh, a visiting priest from India, had been hiding, and shot him in the face. Then he shot at three priests huddled in another nearby room. By the time Page finally fled the temple, six people were dead and several others wounded.

An Oak Creek Police lieutenant, Brian Murphy, fifty-one, had been with the department for twenty-one years and was just five from retirement. He was working a supervisor shift on what had been a calm, beautiful Sunday morning when the wave of frantic 911 calls began pouring in around 10:25 a.m. First that there had been a fight at the Sikh temple, then that shots were fired, and then that there was an active shooter. Realizing he was likely the officer closest to the scene, Murphy raced toward the temple.

The lieutenant arrived two minutes later, saw the Singh brothers dead near the entrance, and then spotted Page come running out of the temple. Both men fired their weapons. The officer missed. The attacker did not—his bullet piercing Murphy's chin and traveling down through his neck.

The severely wounded officer ducked behind a car, but Page snuck up behind him again, shooting the gun out of Murphy's hand. "He didn't look enraged," Murphy, who, miraculously, survived, would later tell the *Milwaukee Journal Sentinel*. "I kept expecting an expression of some sort but . . . it was very deadpan." Page kept firing, pumping three bullets into the officer's bulletproof vest and another twelve into his body before finally becoming distracted by the arrival of a second responding officer. Page and the second officer exchanged several rounds of gunfire before Page turned his gun on himself and pulled the trigger.

Oak Creek mayor Steve Scaffidi was in his backyard on his hands and knees, covered in dirt, when he got the call from the city's fire chief about a shooting at the Sikh temple. A few minutes later came another call, this one from the police chief, who had been a close friend of his for years. Officer Brian Murphy, who Scaffidi had just had a meeting with the week prior, had been shot, the chief told him. The mayor dashed into the shower and then made his way to city hall, where he called several other city officials to fill them in, before heading to the scene.

Scaffidi was just four months into the job of running this suburb of Milwaukee, with a population of roughly thirty-seven thousand. "The darkness of that day is something that lives with you forever," he told me when we spoke on the phone. "After, like, six months, I was looking back on this and saying, 'How the hell did this happen here?'"

Oak Creek sees very little violence, much less mass shootings. The mayor had very little experience with the city's Sikh community, his only direct interaction having come a few years earlier as an alderman, when the temple requested new permits in order to expand its site. He was broadly aware of white supremacists but hadn't ever imagined one would commit a terrorist attack in his city.

For the next eight hours, Scaffidi worked out of a command center set up outside the temple, getting briefings from his police chief and the FBI, and fielding national media calls. And sometime in the late afternoon, not long after he'd briefed the media, the mayor answered a call from a blocked number and was told by the White House switchboard to hold for the president of the United States. He doesn't remember much of the specifics of the call, other than that President Obama spoke in measured, reassuring sentences, as he himself tried to remain composed.

A few hours later, after midnight, Harpreet's family finally received a call of their own, relaying the news he'd been dreading.

The temple had remained a crime scene, and worried family members, including Harpreet's brother and father, had begun to gather with others in the basement of a bowling alley just outside the crime scene tape. An official with the FBI finally called to let them know that Paramjit Kaur had been among the victims. The two men drove home in near silence and relayed the news to Harpreet. They all hugged and cried.

In the weeks to come, Mayor Scaffidi would spend each day in briefings with the FBI, learning about the Hammerskins and the broader white supremacist movement. For the months to follow, he and other city leaders would hold monthly community meetings aimed at passing along what they were learning to the city's equally stunned populace. "We all kind of got educated together," he told me. City officials also held daily meetings with the Sikh elders every day for two weeks following the shootings. And soon, the local Sikhs had begun showing up at community events, asking how they could become more involved.

Harpreet and Kamal became regulars at these public events honoring the slain. At home, they constructed a small shrine memorializing their mother, which included the shoes she'd worn that day, some of her jewelry, and a photo. "She was the sweetest thing you ever could meet," Harpreet told me, still fighting back tears nearly a decade after the attack.

Many in Oak Creek had been shocked to learn that none of the slain would be included in federal hate crime statistics. Even after the rise in violence toward Sikhs in the decade since 9/11, the incomplete federal hate crime data, reliant primarily on self-reported statistics from local police departments, did not include Sikhs among its victim categories.

And so, about one month after the massacre, Harpreet traveled to Washington. Members of the Sikh Coalition, an activist group, had put together a campaign to have crimes against Sikhs added to the federal data. They were determined that those slain in Oak Creek not be erased from the official record. "Heck no!" Harpreet initially responded when he was asked to speak during the congressional hearing that had been called on the issue. But Kamal pushed him to do it. One of them should do this, so their mother's death wouldn't be in vain. Harpreet was the better English speaker of the two, but still feared messing up or stumbling over his words in front of such a large audience. "It's for Mom," Kamal begged. "They will listen, trust me."

Harpreet had never traveled out of state before. He sat nervously through a morning of meetings with various members of Congress. Finally, it came time for him to appear in front of the Senate subcommittee hearing on hate crimes—becoming the first Sikh to ever testify before Congress. He tightened his tie and made sure his turban was sitting straight atop his head and made his way to the hearing room.

"I'm here on behalf of all of the children who lost parents or grandparents during the massacre in Oak Creek, Wisconsin," Harpreet told the committee, reading slowly from his prepared remarks. "Senators, I came here today to ask the government to give my mother the dignity of being a statistic. The FBI does not track hate crimes against Sikhs. My mother and those shot that day will not even count on a federal form. We cannot solve a problem we refuse to recognize," he told the committee. "I also ask that the government pursue domestic terrorists with the same vigor as attacks from abroad."

It would take another year of campaigning, but in August 2013 Attorney General Eric Holder announced that the FBI would expand its hate crime statistics to now include Hindus, Arab Americans, Buddhists, Mormons, Jehovah's Witnesses, Orthodox Christians, and Sikhs.

THE SIKHS IN WISCONSIN HADN'T had time yet to bury, much less mourn, those slain in Oak Creek, when researchers Robert Futrell and Pete Simi heard from an editor at the *New York Times*'s opinion page.

The massacre was the latest in a wave of mass shootings, tucked between Aurora and Newtown, also in 2012, and was at that point the deadliest attack on an American house of worship since the white supremacist 1963 Birmingham, Alabama, church bombing that killed four black schoolgirls. Now the nation wanted to understand *why*. The researchers agreed to author something and hopped on the phone to plan out their *Times* piece.

The duo had spent years researching American white supremacists and coauthored *American Swastika: Inside the White Power Movement's Hidden Spaces of Hate*. In a series of case studies, they explored the various factions of the movement—from Klansmen, to Christian Identity groups such as the Aryan Nations, to neo-Nazis, to racist skinhead groups—and examined the core doctrine through which these groups are intertwined: the belief that the white race is genetically and culturally superior to other races and thus entitled to rule over them.

"So much of the narrative has been dominated by this idea that people are surprised," Futrell, a sociologist at the University of Nevada, told me. "They were surprised about Charlottesville. They were surprised that there were these youngish men in polos. They just didn't look like white supremacists. And we've been super frustrated with that narrative because to those who had been watching this stuff, there is no surprise to it at all. It's not new at all. This movement takes on different forms visually but at its root has the same fundamental ideas."

Among the key findings of Futrell and Simi's research was that the 2008 election of Barack Obama had left much of the movement desperate and despondent.

"From their vantage point, this is their worst nightmare coming to fruition," Simi, now a criminologist at Chapman University in Orange, California, told me. "It's 'We've been talking about this, and now it has actually happened! There is no return now!' The Obama presidency becomes emblematic for all of this stuff they've been speculating and talking about for years. 'It's here! What more proof do you need than the fact that we elected a black guy!'"

For decades, white supremacists had predicted that integration, multiracial families, and growing racial and ethnic diversity would bring about the end of the white race. They had already been enraged by census projections forecasting that in a matter of decades the United States would become a majority-minority nation. And now, the overwhelming popular election of a black president clearly codified "how far a white nation has succumbed to the suicidal stupidity of integration."

"The most central aspect of their worldview is this sense of whiteness and white people being embattled and up against the ropes. In a way, it's a kind of underdog mentality," Simi explained, noting that the theme of the white underdog has long been present in American popular culture, from Sylvester Stallone's *Rocky* to much of the narratives told through Bruce Springsteen's rasp. "That underdog mentality is generally appealing to people."

It's essential to note that this white replacement theory—the central tenet of the U.S. white supremacist movement—is as false today as it is historically and scientifically baseless. There is no biologically distinctive white race to be eliminated. With regard to our socially understood concepts of race and whiteness, there are hundreds of millions of "white people" across the globe—any alleged centuries-long effort to eradicate them has been a remarkable failure. To the extent that a genocide has ever been orchestrated on American soil, it is the subjugation and isolation of the Native peoples who populated this land long before the waves of white immigrants set foot on the continent. Those who advance replacement theory would have you believe that the Jews have masterminded this ever-lurking global conspiracy. Of course, no such conspiracy has ever existed.

As part of their work, Futrell and Simi studied white supremacist gathering places where the movement's foot soldiers are indoctrinated, from skinhead house parties to neo-Nazi Bible studies. They took particular note of the white power music scene.

In recent decades, music has been the tool most integral to the resurgence of the white supremacist movement—at least, that is, until the advent of social media and Internet message boards. Through music, racists have coaxed a generation of desperate white youths into their clutches and proceeded to poison their minds. The songs are often heavy and hard, a cross between punk and metal, played at house shows and, when they can find an establishment sympathetic to the cause, basement bars. The lyrics, often scream-sung, tug as much at the listeners' need for camaraderie as they appeal to their darkest desires.

"Punk rock became part of the lives of its devotees in a way that outsiders, especially adults, never understood. It spoke to us and allowed us to speak when we didn't feel we had a voice. It was uncensored and raw and proved it was okay to be lonely or angry or confused about being a teenager in the world," recalls Christian Picciolini, a notorious skinhead and leader of a hate band who later left the movement, in his memoir *White American Youth: My Descent into America's Most Violent Hate Movement—and How I Got Out*. "I became too engrossed in the energy of the music itself," he reflects. One such example is Skrewdriver, a notorious hate punk band from Britain that was instrumental in seducing Picciolini into the movement. "And I barely registered their lyrics."

As is often the case in major breaking news, details of the Oak Creek shooting trickled out drop by drop. When the *Times* called, Futrell and Simi had heard reports that the gunman had been influenced by, and perhaps even directly involved in, the white power music scene. And so they began to draft an article that would explain the draw of white power music, of the way its lyrics first indoctrinate listeners before propelling them deeper into hatred and closer to violence.

Simi headed to the Southern Poverty Law Center website to see what, if anything else, he could find out about the shooter. At this point they still didn't know his name. That's when he saw the photo.

It was a side profile shot, pulled by the SPLC from the shooter's Myspace page. In it, the man wore a red tank top that showed off his heavily tattooed arms and back. Most prominent was the one etched in thick black ink on his left shoulder: a black cross in a circle, one of the most popular neo-Nazi symbols, and a large "14"—a reference to the "14 words" creed that has for decades been sworn to by white supremacists across the country: "We must secure the existence of our people and a future for white children." Simi's eyes scanned up the photo, from the man's tattoos up to his goatee and partially balding head. He recognized him immediately.

"Oh my God!" he exclaimed to Futrell over the phone. "That's Wade."

His coauthor was confused. "*Who* is Wade?" But Simi couldn't yet muster the words to explain. The shooter at the Sikh temple was a skinhead he'd once known well.

• • •

Much is made about the radicalization process of violent extremists: the traumas and dramas of life that made a given person susceptible to hate; the ways in which he was exposed to poisonous ideology; and then the crisis—the breaking point—that prompted the radical to carry out his chosen act of violence. Yet I've found, more often than not, when interviewing people who have devoted their professional lives to understanding perpetrators of racial violence, that they often share a similar, if diametrically opposite, radicalization process. They can identify the very moment their eyes were opened—when they first realized they'd never again look away from the evil they now saw.

Simi still remembers the first time he witnessed white racism. He was nine years old when he and his mother spent an evening watching a PBS documentary on the resurgence of the Ku Klux Klan. Where, his young mind wondered, do such hateful people come from? Are they born this way, or are they created?

From that point forward, Simi was particularly attuned to racism and was stunned by how often he casually encountered it. The following year, his family moved to suburban Portland. During one of his first neighborhood baseball games, he overheard another young boy singing a dark version of a children's song: "I was walking through the jungle and what did I see? / One hundred and one niggers looking at me." The summer before his sophomore year of high school, Simi was sitting in a friend's living room watching the film *Colors*, the police procedural starring Sean Penn and Robert Duvall, when the friend's father, a prominent community member, responded to one of the movie's black characters by blurting out, "We should flush all the niggers down the toilet."

The N-word was not uncommon in the halls of Simi's middle school and high school. One time, he remembers, a white classmate drew a picture of a lynching and put it on the locker of one of their black classmates. It wasn't a controversy. Just a thing that happened. By his sophomore year, several classmates had become full-blown skinheads, including some boys he'd played sports with. "A lot of other kids accepted them. That stuck with me," Simi recalls. "When does this type of hatred become something that we say is not acceptable? Where is the line?"

Portland, and all of Oregon, has a deep history of racism, much like the rest of the country. In 1844 the territory's government passed a law ordering all black residents to leave or face public flogging. Five year later, a follow-up law prohibited black Americans from entering the territory. When Oregon adopted a state constitution at the end of the following decade, the document explicitly aimed to create an all-white state, forbidding black Americans from residing in, traveling to, or owning property there. Even once the post–Civil War constitutional amendments outlawing slavery and granting black men the right to vote were ratified, Oregon remained a state with very few black residents. And those who did call it home faced open hostility and violence. In the early 1900s the state claimed the highest KKK membership per capita in the union.

By the time Simi's family moved there in the 1980s, Portland had become ground zero for the white supremacist movement. It was dubbed "Skinhead City" because racist skinhead gangs and *anti*-racist skinhead gangs—which are exactly what it sounds like: groups of shaved-head anti-racists—would often do battle in the streets. In 1986 a group of twenty racist skinheads marched through the city's Old Town District armed with pipes, clubs, and axes. Two years later, a group of skinheads nearly stomped an Asian man to death in front of his wife and children.

By then, Portland's growing cadre of young racists had attracted the attention of Tom Metzger, a former Ku Klux Klan grand dragon who in 1983 founded the White Aryan Resistance, a violent neo-Nazi group. Metzger dispatched a recruiter there to help organize a skinhead gang called East Side White Pride—its primary activities consisted of handing out racist tracts and beating up nonwhites. And, on November 13, 1988, three of the group's members would commit one of the nation's most notorious hate crimes.

Ken Mieske, Kyle Brewster, and Steve Strasser had spent much of the night handing out racist tracts downtown and then drinking beers with their skinhead brethren. But as they drove home, they spotted Mulugeta Seraw, a twenty-eight-year-old Ethiopian man who had come to the United States to attend college, standing next to a red Oldsmobile that was idling on a residential street. It was a tight squeeze, and, in order to continue down the road, the skinheads needed the Ethiopians to back their car up. Words were exchanged—politely, and then, much less so. The skinheads leapt from their car, screaming racial slurs and smashing the Oldsmobile's windows with a baseball bat.

"I could see from the back seat: the bat being swung; a man falling to the ground—and then everybody running," Julie Sanders, Mieske's then-girlfriend, a sixteen-year-old skinhead herself when she witnessed the murder, would recall decades later. "The man died. He was born in Ethiopia and had a son. But we just saw 'black.'"

The skinheads initially claimed that the Ethiopians started the fight, but ultimately all three pleaded guilty and were shipped off to prison. And Seraw's killing provided an opening for the Southern Poverty Law Center to sue Metzger, on the grounds that he had directly incited the murder. A jury agreed, awarding Seraw's estate $12.5 million—effectively bankrupting Metzger and his hate group. And lawmakers in Oregon passed what was then one of the most sweeping hate crimes bills in the nation, requiring local police departments to collect and report data on racially motivated crimes.

"The city was in an uproar. The first bulletins were followed by such intense news coverage it was almost as if racism itself, and not only the skinheads movement was being discovered," journalist Elinor Langer recounted in her book *A Hundred Little Hitlers: The Death of a Black Man, the Trial of a White Racist, and the Rise of the Neo-Nazi Movement in America*, the definitive account of Seraw's murder and the legal proceedings that followed. "At supermarkets, bus stops, and lunch counters, the incident was the talk of the town."

The crime held a mirror to Portland, prompting predictably divergent reactions in various parts of a relatively segregated city. Many white Portlanders were shocked by what they saw in the glass: a city where bands of racist skinheads roamed the streets and terrorized immigrants and other people of color. Black residents were incensed but not surprised. Their white neighbors were now seeing Portland precisely as prejudiced as they'd always known it to be.

As Simi followed the news coverage, he was struck by the identities of the attackers. The ringleader, Mieske, had been the homecoming king at a nearby high school, while Brewster was the son of a well-known and highly regarded civic activist. These murderous skinheads seemed no different from his own skinhead classmates. It would have been easy for Simi, a white teen in the suburbs, to believe that racism and white supremacy were either theoretical threats or historical concepts, best left to activists and documentaries; to deem their urgency overstated and banish further contemplation of them from his mind. The skinheads weren't coming for him, after all.

But he couldn't lie to himself. Simi knew now that this hatred was real, a present force in the world that he'd soon inhabit as an adult. Having seen the hatred up close, he made it his mission to figure out why.

Simi's first attempt at fieldwork was embedding with a white supremacist group that called itself the Rocky Mountain Militia.

The organization had begun as a collection of punk rock skin-heads who evolved into Christian Identitarians. Following the vid-eotaped beating by police of Rodney King, a black man who'd led them on a high-speed chase in Los Angeles in 1991, the group's adherents became convinced that the race war was imminent. They fled their headquarters in Las Vegas and relocated to a plot of land along the border of southern Utah and northern Arizona, where they adopted a paramilitary "militia" structure.

The group made a lot of noise—one of its leaders, Johnny Ban-gerter, was a well-known white supremacist who had picketed gay rights groups in Salt Lake City, threatened to kill Utah senator Orrin Hatch (a conservative), and once proposed taking over Utah's Zion National Park to turn it into a whites-only commune—but the Rocky Mountain Militia carried out little action, and it eventu-ally fizzled out. (In recent years, one of the founders has decried his past racist statements and admitted that, in fact, he is part Jewish.)

In need of a new set of subjects, Simi set his sights on Aryan Nations, which was then one of the country's most powerful white supremacist groups. Founder Richard Butler, an aerospace engi-neer who had moved from California to northern Idaho, envisioned establishing an all-white ethnostate in the Pacific Northwest. The Aryan Nations hosted an annual "congress" gathering of white supremacist groups, skinheads, and neo-Nazis that drew a who's who of American racists, building solidarity across what had been to that point a splintered movement. Simi phoned the "church" that they operated on the compound—the Church of Jesus Christ Christian—and asked if he could come visit.

"Are you white?" asked the woman on the other end of the phone.

"Yes," Simi replied.

"Then you're more than welcome."

After his trip to Idaho, Simi turned his attention to the racist skinhead movement. By the late 1990s, the skinheads of Southern California were notorious nationwide for their vicious violence. In the preceding decade, they had carried out attacks on blacks, Jews, and immigrants, and been implicated in crimes such as the murder of Seraw in Portland. They also made defiant national television appearances: white supremacist skinheads started a brawl with a black civil rights activist on the popular daytime talk show *Geraldo*, hosted by Geraldo Rivera, and made an hourlong appearance on *The Oprah Winfrey Show* in which they claimed whites were fundamentally superior to blacks, advocated racial violence, and called Winfrey a "monkey" to her face.

The groups would later use the television clips as recruitment tools, and Winfrey has said that she regrets ever inviting them on, describing it as one of the most important lessons she ever learned in broadcasting. "I realized in that moment that I was doing more to empower them than to expose them," she said in 2011. "What I thought I had been doing had been allowing people to see how violent, how abusive, how not smart they were. I was actually doing the opposite." It was these same California skinheads who were fictionalized and depicted in the 1998 movie *American History X*, in which Edward Norton plays a reformed neo-Nazi desperate to extract his kid brother from the movement.

By the time Simi began his fieldwork, the most notorious skinheads had aged out of their teens and were approaching their midthirties. He set out to track them down and find out if they were still in the movement or if new wisdom had come with age, and they'd abandoned their racist ideologies.

One of the skinheads Simi found lived in an old townhouse in the city of Orange, in Orange County. He'd been a member of the WarSkins, a racist skinhead group, and was skeptical of Simi. The two emailed back and forth for more than a year before he agreed to let the researcher visit.

"He sends me his phone number and gives me an address. It's an old convenience store with a phone booth out front," Simi recalled. "He has me call the number from the phone booth—turns out his house was across the street. He did this whole cloak-and-dagger thing before finally saying, 'I'm across the street on the porch. Come over.'"

It was a slow, calculated process, with Simi hesitant to dive too deeply or too quickly into his questions, for fear of scaring off his subjects. He would act as a fly on the wall. The goal was to understand the natural course of their lives; to see, up close, how America's avowed racists live day in and day out. If they headed out to a restaurant or beach, Simi followed. When they had house parties or attended punk rock shows, Simi was there. And, as they did often, when the guys were sitting around on the couch drinking beer and watching television, Simi was there sipping a beer of his own.

A lesson learned early in his studies was not to delve quickly into personal details with his subjects. Instead, Simi was just *there*, letting these men become comfortable with his presence and small talk. Rarely did he conduct formal interviews. His insights into their worldviews and lives were pieced together by listening to hours of their passing remarks, studiously jotted down in his notebook.

That first night, they all went to an old VFW bar to play darts. Once Simi's presence was explained, one of the skinhead's friends exclaimed, "Oh, he wants to study us!" During a subsequent visit, however, another local skinhead demanded an official letter, on university letterhead, to prove that the researcher wasn't secretly a federal agent.

But the process was working, with Simi slowly building the trust of his subjects over the course of a half dozen or so trips. Until one time Simi showed up on the doorstep for an agreed-upon weekend visit, and an unknown man answered the door. The contact hadn't had any roommates previously, and he'd never seen this guy before. He asked for his contact by name. "Nah, he's still at work," explained the young man, who offered up that he was a new roommate.

So, Simi explained that he had come into town for the weekend, and that the plan was to stay here at the house. Would it be all right if he sat on the couch to wait?

"Oh, come on in," said the man—whose name, Simi would soon learn, was Wade Michael Page.

When Simi first met him, Page was working a few shifts a week at a local sandwich shop. But eventually he lost that job, and he was routinely underemployed and largely leeching off of his friends. While he'd come to study Page's roommate, Simi ended up spending most of his time with Wade. The men got along well. They were about the same age and liked similar music—Rush, Pearl Jam, Nirvana—the type of mainstream stuff that a lot of racist skinheads had sworn off.

Unlike so many of his compatriots, Page didn't have a particularly violent history: a few arrests, yes, but they were almost exclusively alcohol related. In fact, during the time they'd spent together, Simi watched as Page abstained from his friends' violent acts. One night a skinhead who'd recently been released from prison started a bar fight during a game of pool. Most of the group found themselves sucked into the brawl, but Page stayed out of the fray, leaning back against the barroom wall. Sure, he read violent white supremacist propaganda. But he was never the guy at the party declaring drunkenly, "We need to start the race war! Tonight!"

To be clear, Page *was* an out-and-out racist; he wasn't spending all of his time hanging out with skinheads and neo-Nazis for the free beer. Page tossed around the N-word and ranted about how blacks were prone to criminality and sponged on society. He proudly hated Jews, gays, liberals, and what he considered to be Communists. One time Page, his roommate, and Simi went to a local pizza shop. It was during the winter holidays, and the restaurant had a Hanukkah menorah hanging from the door. Both Page and his roommate refused to touch the door, and contemplated leaving, until Simi offered to open the door so that neither would have to risk touching a Jewish symbol. At another lunch, the group was served by a friendly and attractive waitress who appeared to be Asian. When she walked away after taking their orders, Simi posed a question to the group: Would they consider dating someone like her? Page reacted with disgust. "*Of course not!*"

Toward the end of our first conversation, I asked Simi a question I knew he'd fielded before: Would he ever have imagined that, of all of the white supremacists he'd studied and gotten to personally know over the years, Wade Page would be the one to commit a racist mass shooting?

In response, Simi told me a story of a night, decades earlier, when he and Page had gone out drinking and found themselves shooting pool against two other men, one of whom was black. "How do you feel about what we just did?" Simi asked afterward. "Well, if I had it my way, we'd all be living separately," Page replied. "But that's not the world we live in."

Simi paused as he recounted that night. Page, he told me, could have found a way out; his story didn't have to end the way it did. Still, he continued, it's never a surprise when someone who has committed themselves to a violent ideology of hate ends up acting on those beliefs.

"When you get involved with these types of groups, one of the most dangerous things about it is that everyone becomes capable of this type of violence, because the movement valorizes this type of violence and redefines violence as a form of self-defense," he explained. "They say, 'Look at what they're doing to our race. If we're not violent, we'll cease to exist.'"

14

DARYL JOHNSON'S LIFELONG OBSESSION WITH people like Wade Page began one night in the mid-1980s, when, as a fifteen-year-old, he was flipping through TV channels and landed on a newscast covering an armed standoff in Arkansas.

Federal law enforcement had surrounded the hideout of a white supremacist group called the Covenant Sword of the Lord. Convinced that doomsday was imminent, the group had constructed a paramilitary compound and begun training to violently overthrow the United States government. The Covenant was a Christian Identity group, a subsection of the white supremacist movement that preaches that northern Europeans are God's chosen people, with close ties to other violent white supremacist organizations. In April 1985 the federal agents surrounded the compound to carry out a search warrant, resulting in a multiday standoff that ultimately ended without any shots fired and a massive cache of weapons and explosives seized.

Johnson was hooked and would spend the next two decades learning more about right-wing extremist groups. He went off to Brigham Young University in Utah, where he studied criminal justice. During a Mormon mission in Michigan, he studied the local militia groups. And ultimately he went off to work in counterterrorism. He spent five years working for the U.S. Bureau of Alcohol, Tobacco, Firearms and Explosives (ATF) before, in 2005, transferring to the Department of Homeland Security, with a specific focus on domestic terror and white supremacists. "The first year, I was the only guy working these types of issues," Johnson recalled. "They said, 'We want to have this expertise, but right now we're still focusing on Al Qaeda.'"

In the United States, it's relatively easy to commit an act of terror due to the wide availability of firearms. As mass shooting after mass shooting has demonstrated, a single individual can inflict carnage, claiming dozens and even hundreds of people as victims in just a matter of minutes. Yet right-wing domestic extremists and white supremacists have additionally benefited from the federal government's intense focus on international terrorism and hesitance to actively monitor its white citizens.

Americans have the right to hold and proselytize repugnant, racist beliefs. And unlike with foreign extremists, whose membership in or support of formally designated terrorist groups means they've often already committed a crime, law enforcement often has no pretext for monitoring and disrupting many domestic white supremacist groups until *after* they've already carried out an act of violence.

The most pressing question of this era may be how to balance the rights of Americans—even American racists—to free speech and free expression with the government's sacred responsibility to ensure the safety and security of the rest of society. For nearly thirty years, terrorism experts have warned, with increasing levels of alarm, about the growing threat of white supremacist terrorists. And yet for nearly thirty years, the federal government has largely looked in the other direction.

On April 19, 1995, twenty-six-year-old Timothy McVeigh drove a rented Ryder moving van filled with homemade explosives up to the Alfred P. Murrah Federal Building in Oklahoma City, put it in park, and walked away as the bomb detonated. When the carnage cleared, the building was destroyed, and 168 people were dead, including 19 children.

While McVeigh insisted that he was not a member of any movement or political group and that his coconspirators had not been violently coerced by him, there was ample evidence that he was, in fact, a member of the white supremacist movement. He'd spent time around militia members in both Arizona and Michigan. The choice of the federal building had previously been targeted by Richard Snell, a white supremacist who'd been convicted of two murders and was slated to be executed on the day of McVeigh's attack. During the fifty-one-day standoff in Waco, Texas, between federal agents and the Branch Davidians in 1993, McVeigh had traveled there to witness the scene in person, perching on the hood of his car and selling bumper stickers that read "Fear the Government That Fears Your Gun, Politicians Love Gun Control" and "Ban Guns, Make the Streets Safe for a Government Takeover." He read and shared white supremacist writings, including *The Turner Diaries*, a 1978 novel written by white supremacist William Luther Pierce under the nom de plume Andrew Macdonald that is perhaps the most widely read racist propaganda of our time.

The book is written as a diary by Earl Turner, a fictional soldier in what white supremacists believe will be the coming revolution to overthrow multiracial democracy. Turner and his collaborators undertake increasingly violent acts in hopes of radicalizing more of their fellow white citizens in the buildup to the coming war. "One of the major purposes of political terror, always and everywhere, is to force the authorities to take reprisals and to become more repressive, thus alienating a portion of the population and generating sympathy for the terrorists," Turner writes.

Ultimately, Turner and his fellow white supremacists come to the realization that the masses, who they believe have been manipulated by the mass media, will never "wake up" to their message and, in turn, begin carrying out assassinations and mass bombings. They bomb FBI headquarters, killing seven hundred people. Then they raid the newsroom of the *Washington Post* and murder the editorial page editor. At one point, the book depicts a bombing much like the one McVeigh would ultimately carry out. "There is no way we can destroy the System without hurting many thousands of innocent people," Turner explains.

The bombing and McVeigh's arrest rocked the nation, aiming a spotlight at the growing antigovernment militia movement, and prompting law enforcement and the administration of the new president, Bill Clinton, to devote further resources to preventing acts of terrorism. It was the moment, in the last half century, when both the political class and the citizenry were most singularly focused on the threat presented by white supremacist terror. But that moment would soon pass, as they always do.

In June 1995 Senator Arlen Specter of Pennsylvania, a declared candidate in the upcoming Republican presidential primary, called a hearing to explore the danger presented by the burgeoning militia movement. Since the Oklahoma City bombing, militia leaders had become mainstays of mainstream political coverage, as reporters sought to understand the world from which McVeigh was believed to have come and to explain why he might have carried out his act of terror.

"The militias were growing and active long before Oklahoma City. Their internal publications and instructional videos are filled with the language of hate and with paranoid conspiracy theories," Senator Carl Levin, of Michigan, told the committee.

Levin's state has long been perceived as a hotbed of militia activity. Both McVeigh and coconspirator Terry Nichols, who was imprisoned for life due to his involvement in the Oklahoma City bombing, "had connections with an extremist militia group called the Wolverine Watchmen"—the same group whose members would be arrested in 2020 and charged with hatching a plot to kill Michigan governor Gretchen Whitmer.

"People have the right to say hateful things and believe hateful things about their government, but that doesn't make it right to say them," Levin continued. "Extreme hate rhetoric contributes to an incendiary atmosphere in which an unstable individual will take the rhetoric seriously and light a match or a fuse."

Witnesses from local and federal law enforcement testified that the threat of such militia groups had grown more intense in recent years, attributable in part to a 1992 FBI standoff with white supremacist Randy Weaver in Ruby Ridge, Idaho, and the massacre of the Branch Davidians in Waco, Texas. These groups, they testified, drew their membership from those skeptical of the federal government, angered by taxation and the use of presidential executive orders, and those propelled by racial prejudice toward immigrants, black Americans, and Jews. Each of the five law enforcement officials present described militias as "disturbing" or "dangerous."

"Federal and local enforcement personnel have been threatened, harassed, assaulted, and shot by militia members," testified James L. Brown, a deputy associate director at the ATF.

"Maricopa County, which includes Phoenix, has seen in the recent past a tremendous increase in white supremacist groups," added Richard Romley, a prosecutor from Arizona. "What is probably the most troubling, and without getting into all the very specific comments, is that the comments are becoming more violent in nature with specific threats of doing bodily harm, as well as causing death, and that is a major concern."

"We see a lot of concern out there, a lot of misinformation," said Fred M. Mills, superintendent of the Missouri State Highway Patrol. "We see a lot of individuals who are really and truly, I think, just simply misguided, and again they see this as an opportunity to come to the forefront and expound those hate philosophies and carry out their acts."

It's hard to revisit the transcript of the day's hearing and not think it reads much like a congressional hearing held today with witnesses speaking on behalf of QAnon conspiracy theories and the white supremacist movement. Law enforcement officials who had dealt with the groups directly issuing dire warnings. The summoned group leaders insisting it was unfair to paint their entire organizations as racist and protesting that their grievances are legitimate. A group of senators sitting there, seemingly skeptical of everyone.

Five militia leaders were brought before the committee, where they testified that "lesbians" and "sex perverts" were running the FBI and IRS, the military was building "civilian prison camps" on army bases, and the United Nations was controlling the weather. One of them went on to speculate that it was really the Japanese behind the Oklahoma City bombing. Another claimed that there was not enough evidence to rule out that the bombing hadn't been part of a larger conspiracy, comparing it to the John F. Kennedy assassination. Another complained about political correctness and law enforcement overreach. They compared themselves to the revolutionaries of the thirteen colonies rising up against a tyrannical government. The federal government, one militiaman declared, needed a "spanking."

James Johnson, a spokesperson for Ohio Unorganized Militia, testified: "The national news media and the actions of this government is some of the best recruitment we could have. . . . The animosity that I see out there between the citizens and the government is frightening." Johnson, a black man, was the only nonwhite militia member to testify.

"Two hundred years ago," he went on, "the British didn't get the hint until they saw dead redcoats out there. This time, maybe we can get this out in the open and have things resolved because I feel—and it's concerning to me, and I'm being sincerely honest—with the increasing polarization between the taxpaying public out

there and what goes on not only in here but certain state governments that the only thing standing between some of the current
legislation being contemplated and armed conflict is time."

The purpose of the hearings, as Senator Specter told one of the
militia members, was to "expose" the beliefs of these groups to the
public—although likely also very much about keeping his own
name in the headlines—without much consideration for whether
such exposure would have its intended effect of turning off the
American people. "I want your ideas fully exposed," Specter declared. "I want your ideas compared to mine, and I want the American public to judge whether you're right or I'm right."

Around the same time the House Judiciary Committee held its own
hearing to debate counterterrorism legislation that the Clinton administration had proposed in response to the bombing. The committee summoned FBI director Louis Freeh and other federal law
enforcement officials to Capitol Hill for questioning.

Toward the beginning of the hearing, Representative John Conyers of Michigan, the committee's ranking Democrat, said, "The
first thing that I want to do is indicate that I am probably very nervous about us proceeding in the environment that we're in; namely,
that we're grieving over the Oklahoma City bombing. We've sworn
to take action, and we have moved rather expeditiously, but, you
know, at the same time, I may be the only member here that was
around when we were worried about what J. Edgar Hoover and the
FBI were doing in the spying on the NAACP and other civil rights
activities. That wasn't that long ago. We then went through that
period of Americans being harassed during the Vietnam War. And
so what I'm concerned about is that we would allow federal investigators to target Americans of particular political beliefs, and that
takes us back to the bad old days."

Conyers's anxiety, and that of other black members of Congress,
was well founded in history. The FBI had used its investigative

power to aggressively monitor and disrupt black civil rights groups and activists that it deemed radical—and these were far from the only hard questions being asked about the new counterterrorism proposal.

Representative Charles Schumer, then a Democratic House member from New York, raised a crucial question that surfaces (or at least should surface) each time law enforcement blames its failure to prevent an attack on a lack of resources. Of all of the money the FBI was spending, how much of it was going to preventing terror? Freeh responded that of the several hundred people working on FBI counterterrorism, "a very large majority are devoted to international terrorism as opposed to domestic." The FBI director vowed that would change, especially if Congress approved additional funding.

Representative Steven Schiff, a Republican from New Mexico, scrutinized the proposed Counterterrorism Center, which would come with an additional one thousand employees. "I think it's remarkable that in the administration's budget proposal that was submitted only a couple of months ago none of this was included or mentioned," Schiff told Freeh. "I'm wondering why, if there was a need for this number of people to fight counterterrorism, to fight terrorism rather as counterterrorism, if you can explain to me why the administration didn't think they were important about two months ago."

Of chief concern to some on the committee was the suggestion that the FBI could begin wiretapping or otherwise monitoring U.S. citizens based on their political ideology. Under guidelines set by Congress, the agency was able to order a wiretap on someone suspected of some federal crimes, but not all of them. Now the bureau was asking for a more expansive list of crime investigations that could prompt this type of surveillance, including crimes such as tax evasion. "So, if people get together and protest taxes and jump up and down and say they're not going to pay their taxes but really are paying their taxes, are you going to subject them to federal wiretaps?" asked Representative Bobby Scott of Virginia, a Democrat. That was not how it would work, Freeh insisted.

One year and one week after the bombings, President Bill Clinton signed the Antiterrorism and Effective Death Penalty Act of 1996 into law. Included in the final legislation was an additional $1 billion in funding for counterterrorism efforts and a provision limiting the number of appeals that could be filed by federal death row inmates as well as other incarcerated people. Missing from the bill was the request for expanding federal wiretap authority. In 2000 the Clinton administration gave way to the presidency of George W. Bush. Just nine months into his first term, on September 11, 2001, nineteen terrorist hijackers affiliated with the Islamic terrorist group Al Qaeda flew airplanes into the World Trade Center in New York as well as the Pentagon (a fourth plane, headed to Washington, crash-landed in Pennsylvania), leaving nearly three thousand dead and forever altering the way Americans conceptualize the threat of terrorism.

The Department of Homeland Security, established after the 9/11 terror attacks, is a mega-agency charged with, among other things, overseeing immigration and border enforcement, natural disaster response, the Coast Guard, Transportation Security Administration (TSA), and Secret Service, and coordinating the country's counterterrorism efforts. Yet former DHS leaders readily admit that in its early years the department focused its counterterrorism efforts primarily on Islamic terrorism and not homegrown extremists.

"9/11 was a big preoccupation," Michael Chertoff, who ran DHS from 2005 to 2009, told me. It wasn't as if the new agency ignored the threat posed by white supremacists—for example, it extracted guilty pleas to mail fraud and filing a false tax return from Klan leader David Duke, earning him fifteen months in federal prison. But the department's mandate, as it related to terrorism, was clear: prevent another 9/11. "Much of the intelligence we were collecting was focused on transnational terrorist groups."

That's not to say no one was sounding the alarm. In 2005, Democrats on the House Homeland Security Committee issued a report on the tenth anniversary of the Oklahoma City bombing expressing concern that the DHS's five-year budget plan "failed to mention right-wing domestic terrorist groups in its list of terrorist threats facing the United States. . . .

"FBI officials say right-wing militants—including skinheads, neo-Nazis, violent militia members, and the so-called Christian Patriot movement—now pose America's most serious domestic terrorist threat. In fact, white supremacists, traditionally the most violent right-wing group, have strengthened their recruiting and rhetoric since 9/11," the Democrats wrote.

"According to a recent news article, DHS distributed a January 2005 budgetary planning document titled 'Integrated Planning Guidance, Fiscal Years 2005–2011,' which identified certain domestic terror groups as posing potential threats to the homeland. Given the FBI's designation of right-wing groups as 'the most serious domestic threat,' it is surprising that, according to the article, DHS's planning document did not name right-wing domestic terrorists or terrorist groups as a potential threat. However, the document reportedly does list left-wing domestic groups . . . as terrorist threats."

The report quoted Michael German, a recently retired FBI agent who had spent much of his career infiltrating right-wing groups, as saying: "They are still a threat, and they will continue to be a threat. If for some reason the government no longer considers them a threat, I think they will regret that. Hopefully it's an oversight."

Yet the House Democrats' report landed with a thud at the DHS. They were in the minority, after all. And even at the FBI, which had listed right-wing terror as a growing threat, the chief concern remained Islamic terror. A U.S. Justice Department audit would later find that from 2005 to 2009, out of almost 2,000 agents assigned to work counterterrorism, just 330 on average were working domestic cases.

"There is enormous sensitivity against triggering investigations against American citizens for extremism," Chertoff told me. But, he acknowledged, the factors that drive this type of right-wing extremism have only intensified in the last decade and a half. "There's a much wider set of authorities for collecting intelligence on foreign actors, and it gets more challenging [with domestic terror]. There are different rules about wiretapping, and First Amendment concerns. You're not to be investigating people because they are expressing views that are out of favor . . . really limiting the ability of the government to target domestic political groups."

But, in retrospect, Chertoff acknowledged, it was clear even in the mid-aughts that the United States was seeing increasing levels of Far Right radicalization, as the nation grappled with its worst economic crisis since the Depression, the two major political parties became increasingly polarized and hostile in their rhetoric (reflected in the less respectful and more combative tone and nature of political discourse among the public), new waves of immigration reshaped the demographics of various parts of the country, and the advent of the Internet provided a forum for the disaffected to find common cause and camaraderie.

These were the same factors that had fueled prior iterations of the white supremacist movement in the modern era: its post–civil rights, post-Vietnam surge, as well as the rise of the militia and Christian Nationalist organizations of the 1990s. And it would be these same factors, under the presidency of Donald Trump, that would help drive the ascension of the so-called alt-right. "We are in a time when not only is this ideology resurging, partially because of the Internet, but there is a profound cynicism generally about our American institutions," Chertoff told me. "That's a petri dish in which this particular form of bacteria takes off. People feed on that sense of mistrust."

Yet even as that bacteria was proliferating, Daryl Johnson's initial work portfolio was directed primarily at ecoterrorism and threats to the national energy grid. But by 2007, his team had expanded, and his work had begun to diversify. They prepared a report on drug trafficking by racist skinheads and worked with local police agencies to disrupt neo-Nazi groups. By then, Senator Barack Obama's presidential campaign had taken the political world by storm, and it was clear that, for the first time in more than a decade, there was a legitimate shot of a major political party nominating a black American as its presidential nominee. Capitol Police phoned DHS in January 2007, informing the department that Obama was going to launch his presidential bid and asking it to run an analysis of any white supremacist threats against him. There were no major concerns at the time, although plenty of static online. There were at least two foiled plots against Obama during the general election campaign. Then in 2008 the housing bubble burst, the economy was again faltering, and Obama won the presidential election— leaving Johnson afraid for what he suspected would soon come.

The day after Obama's decisive victory over John McCain, Johnson started working on the report that would upend his career.

The 2008 election had prompted new waves of domestic terror and incessant online chatter of more to come. The militia groups of the early 1990s had begun to reform. There was an act of arson at a black church in New England. A mass shooting in Boston committed by a neo-Nazi. Another shooting, a murder-suicide, perpetrated by a white supremacist near Pittsburgh. Then in May 2009 came the murder of George Tiller, a Kansas doctor who ran one of the few clinics in the country that offered late-term abortions. Two weeks later, an eighty-eight-year-old neo-Nazi attempted to shoot up the United States Holocaust Memorial Museum in Washington, DC, killing a black security guard.

On April 7, after nearly two dozen rounds of revisions, the nine-page final report *Rightwing Extremism: Current Economic and Political Climate Fueling Resurgence in Radicalization and Recruitment* went out to law enforcement agencies. Among its key findings were that the economic downturn and the election of a black president "present unique drivers for rightwing radicalization and recruitment" and "could create a fertile recruiting environment for rightwing extremists and even result in confrontations between such groups and government authorities similar to those in the past." The economic and political climate, the authors wrote, "has some similarities to the 1990s, when rightwing extremism experienced a resurgence" and led to more attacks. It went on to say that fears about impending gun restrictions by the Democratic administration and the ongoing public battles over immigration policy could further fuel a rise in right-wing extremism. Yet another factor: the waves of returning war veterans from Iraq and Afghanistan, who, according to the report, made inviting prey for right-wing extremists to "attempt to recruit and radicalize . . . in order to exploit their skills and knowledge derived from military training and combat. . . .

"The willingness of a small percentage of military personnel to join extremist groups during the 1990s because they were disgruntled, disillusioned, or suffering from the psychological effects of war is being replicated today," the report noted. Timothy McVeigh, for instance, had been a veteran of Operation Desert Storm. Further, the report noted, in the years since, both the FBI and civil rights groups had warned of the risk of other military veterans joining white supremacist organizations and extremist groups.

The relatively short report was diagnostic, not prescriptive. It did not advocate any specific law enforcement action be taken. As

Johnson told me, it was intended as an internal heads-up. But the report quickly landed in the hands of Roger Hedgecock, a conservative talk radio host and former mayor of San Diego, and was soon the talk of much of the conservative media. "They objected to the term *right wing*. They equated that to being the Republican Party," Johnson recalled. "People took that out of context and made it sound like we were going to spy on conservatives and Tea Party activists. Some people got offended that we pointed out a connection between returning veterans being targeted for recruitment by these groups." By the time Johnson got into the office the following Monday, it was utter chaos. Every television was turned to Fox News, where every show seemed to feature outrage about Johnson's report.

"She Is Watching You" screamed the banner headline on the influential online conservative political aggregator Drudge Report, next to a picture of Homeland Security Secretary Janet Napolitano. Rush Limbaugh, the most powerful voice in conservative talk radio, told his listeners the report was "nothing more than a partisan hit job filled with lies and innuendo that portrays any conservatism as right-wing extremism."

Driving much of the outrage was the suggestion that returning war veterans could be particularly susceptible. Years later, in the book *Bring the War Home: The White Power Movement and Paramilitary America*, author Kathleen Belew documented how the post-Vietnam period provided a key unification of the white supremacist movement, with its leaders prioritizing the recruitment of disillusioned military veterans—a strategy that continues to this day. Also continuing to this day: the reticence to acknowledge the sensitive proposition that the U.S. military serves as an indispensable pipeline for white supremacist groups looking to fill their ranks.

Most damning for Johnson's report, ultimately, would be the response from the war veterans service organization the American

Legion. Its national commander, David Rehbein, blasted *Rightwing Extremism* in a letter to Napolitano. "I think it is important for all of us to remember that Americans are not the enemy. The terrorists are," he wrote. "To continue to use McVeigh as an example of the stereotypical 'disgruntled military veteran' is as unfair as using Osama bin Laden as the sole example of Islam."

EARLY ONE MORNING, JUST A few days after the Oklahoma City bombing, a ringing telephone startled Janet Napolitano awake. At the other end was the deputy attorney general. Federal authorities had captured Timothy McVeigh. The planning for the attack, it seemed, had taken place in Arizona. By the end of the day, he told the U.S. Attorney for Arizona, she needed to have a fully functional command center in place from which to oversee one of the most extensive federal investigations and prosecutions in American history.

A half decade later, as the state's attorney general, Napolitano would prosecute Frank Roque, the Phoenix man who had driven through the streets in the days following 9/11 looking for Arab Americans to assault—eventually killing a Sikh man working at a local gas station.

The mandate of the DHS is so broad it would be impossible for one person to hold all of the necessary expertise, but by the time President-elect Obama nominated her to run the agency, Napolitano believed she knew enough and could learn the rest. From day one, she told me, she worried about the threat posed by white supremacists. "I was particularly concerned about the safety of President Obama. The memory of 9/11 was still very ripe in people's minds, but we also had an eye on the rise of right-wing extremism."

There was a black president. A faltering economy. A still-ferocious public debate about immigration. The types of people who find themselves attracted to white supremacist and right-wing extremist groups were plenty aggrieved. "When you think about the rise in right-wing extremism, you have to also correlate that with the rise in lone wolves," she told me. The reality then and now is that Louis Beam's fantasy of leaderless resistance has played out. Among the deadliest attackers are so-called lone wolves, who've coordinated their violence with no one but themselves. "They're almost impossible to prevent," she continued. "You don't have a group, so you don't have any communications to intercept. You don't have any opportunity to infiltrate, you don't have somebody who is a member of the group who feels like they've gone too far and tips you off."

But the DHS report had stirred up a hornet's nest in the conservative media, with right-wing groups calling for Napolitano's resignation and Republican elected officials piling on. Most offensive, they claimed, was any insinuation that veterans could be particularly susceptible to such groups' recruitment efforts. "I think Secretary Napolitano has an awful lot of explaining to do," declared House Minority Leader John Boehner. "When you look at this report on right-wing extremism, it includes . . . about two-thirds of Americans, who, you know, who might go to church, who may have served in the military, who may be involved in community activities. It's bizarre."

Although much of the public firestorm raged from the political Right, the Left, too, expressed concerns over the report's language and that its implied solutions were the same types of unconstitutional surveillance long deployed by local and federal law enforcement against Muslims and civil rights groups.

"The way for local police to secure their communities against real threats is to focus on criminal activities and the individuals involved in criminal activities. If these 'intelligence' reports described recent crimes and the people who perpetrated them, there would be little problem from a civil rights perspective," wrote Michael German, who had a decade before testified about the looming threat of white supremacist terror and was now working as a senior policy counsel for the American Civil Liberties Union. Instead, he said, Johnson's study had focused on the same theory of "radicalization" that law enforcement had used to justify spying on Muslims following 9/11. "Actual empirical studies of terrorism conducted in the Netherlands and Britain refute this theory, but the idea that hard-to-find terrorists can be caught by spying on easy-to-find activists appears too hard to resist to U.S. law enforcement. . . .

"Focusing on ideas rather than crime, the latest bulletin from DHS cites an increase in 'rhetoric,' yet doesn't even mention reports that there was a dirty bomb found in an alleged white supremacist's house in Maine last December," he added. "Learning what to look for in that situation might actually be useful to a cop. Threat reports that focus on ideology instead of criminal activity are threatening to civil liberties and a wholly ineffective use of federal security resources."

One week after the report went out, Representative Bennie Thompson, a black Democrat from Mississippi who led the House committee that oversees the DHS budget, sent Napolitano a letter objecting to the report. "This report appears to have blurred the line between violent belief, which is constitutionally protected, and violent action, which is not," Thompson wrote. "I am disappointed and surprised that the department would allow this report to be disseminated."

The following day, Napolitano released a statement, in essence, apologizing for the report, promising to meet with veterans' groups, and insisting that no one would be monitored based solely on ideological beliefs.

"The loose language in the report was interpreted by veterans' groups to suggest that anybody who served in the military was basically a right-wing extremist in waiting. They went ballistic about it," Napolitano told me. "Politics being what it is, and when I read it and read the language that they objected to, I could see their point. And I apologized."

But the political dustup had serious implications for counter-terrorism. The report was fully retracted, and soon the meager resources that had been devoted to addressing domestic terror and right-wing extremism had been diverted. In 2011 the *Washington Post* reported that Johnson's unit had been "effectively eviscerated" and that DHS had canceled state and local law enforcement briefings about domestic terrorism and halted the dissemination of nearly a dozen reports about domestic extremist groups. Napolitano insisted to me that nothing changed fundamentally about how the department investigated domestic right-wing terror, although analysts such as Johnson have spent years pointing back to the controversy surrounding the 2009 report as a key moment in understanding what was to come.

No matter the flaws in his report's wording or recommendations, the decade to follow would see Daryl Johnson's dire predictions about right-wing extremism and white supremacist terror come true. White supremacist groups' ranks swelled throughout the Obama administration and into the Trump years, and a number of high-profile attacks were committed by former military members such as Wade Michael Page. "I don't get any satisfaction or gloating from saying I was right," Johnson told me recently. "Unfortunately, it all got lost in the political melee." He just wishes his bosses had listened to him.

"We could have been even more aggressive in pushing the danger of right-wing extremism and its growth in our society," Napolitano conceded to me. "Certainly being in the military does not cause you to become a right-wing extremist, but the fact is that a number of these acts have been committed by young men who have been in the military, and we need to understand that better."

PART IV

AN AMERICAN NAZI'S FINAL BARK

I imagine one of the reasons people cling to their hates so stubbornly is because they sense, once hate is gone, they will be forced to deal with pain.

—JAMES BALDWIN, *The Fire Next Time*, 1963

16

MINDY CORPORON WASN'T SUPPOSED TO be at the Jewish Community Center of Greater Kansas City in Overland Park, Kansas, that afternoon. She and her husband had taken their twelve-year-old, Lucas, to his weekend lacrosse game. Her own mother, who'd typically be the next option for giving one of the boys a ride, was already booked: it was Palm Sunday, and she was at the local mall having Easter bunny pictures taken with another set of grandkids. And so, the task of driving fourteen-year-old Reat to the JCC for a singing tryout had fallen to her sixty-nine-year-old father, William, a physician.

Her parents had been there from the very beginning, helping her raise Reat after his father left when the boy was just four weeks old. For ten months, Corporon and her newborn lived in her parents' home in Oklahoma, with all three adults playing the role of parent. After Mindy remarried, relocated to Kansas City, and had Lucas, her parents moved too, so they could continue to be close to the boys.

Reat was just two years old when the family realized that the toddler had a God-given talent for performing, using his seemingly photographic memory to capture the choreography of his favorite Disney movies and then reenact them scene for scene. By age four, they'd signed him up for theater, and every summer for the next six years, he acted in a production. At thirteen, Reat got a voice coach and took dance lessons. He landed a role in his school's production of *Damn Yankees* and had just tried out for a community theater production of *Tom Sawyer*.

For years, Reat had waited to be old enough to try out for KC SuperStar, a local *American Idol*–style singing competition. And now, as a high school freshman, he was eligible. By the day of the audition, April 13, 2014, he'd been practicing for a year, preparing to take the stage, picking out his outfit, and perfecting each note. He planned to perform two numbers: "On the Street Where You Live" from the musical *My Fair Lady*, and the Depression-era classic "You're Going to Miss Me When I'm Gone" by the Carter Family. Sometimes, even all these years later, Mindy can still hear Reat singing the lines "When I'm gone, when I'm gone / You're gonna miss me when I'm gone," his voice echoing through the halls of their home.

She felt bad about missing her older son's performance for Lucas's lacrosse game, but Reat insisted she be there to support his younger brother. "Popeye can take me to the audition," he assured his mother. He'd called his grandfather that since before he could fully pronounce words. As it turned out, the lacrosse game ended up canceled. And so, Mindy excitedly drove back across town to the JCC, hoping she'd arrive in time to see Reat's performance.

It was supposed to be a busy day at the JCC. In addition to the KC SuperStar contest, a local stage production of *To Kill a Mockingbird* was scheduled for early that afternoon. The baseball fields a few yards away were set to host an umpire clinic. And, in general, Sundays were always busy at the rec center, as weekend warriors poured in for their workouts.

But Mindy noticed something odd as she pulled into the parking lot: hardly any people. As she looked from left to right, she spotted her father's familiar red truck. Oddly, both the driver's side and passenger doors were open. And then, she spotted her father lying motionless on the ground. As she brought her car to a stop in the parking lot aisle, a few feet from her father's parked truck, she could tell that something terrible had happened. She could feel it.

She leaped from her car, keys in hand, screaming out, "What happened?!" to her father. When she got close enough to really see, she knew there was no point. She couldn't tell what had happened, but as her eyes settled on the pool of blood surrounding his head, she knew he was dead. And in that second, she insisted to me as she recounted it all these years later, Mindy heard a voice telling her that her father was in heaven and that she needed to go find Reat. Mindy walked around the back of the truck, and saw her son, so handsome in the coat and tie he'd worn for the performance, lying in the arms of two men she didn't recognize.

"What happened? What happened?!" the men frantically asked as they tended to Mindy's boy. Then, a third person grabbed Mindy before she could get any closer. "That's my father back there, and he's in heaven," Mindy said, shock beginning to set in. "And that's my son."

From there it all blurs into one hazy memory. The men told her there was a shooter on the loose, then one of them picked her up and carried her inside of the building.

The gunman would make his way down the street, to the parking lot of Village Shalom, a Jewish assisted-living facility. There he encountered fifty-three-year-old Terri LaManno, who had come to visit her mother.

LaManno had grown up in Kansas City, the youngest of five children in a devoted Catholic family. She had been a nurse, giving it up to stay home and raise two children with her husband, Jim, then went back to school to become an occupational therapist and was working at a center for visually impaired children.

"Her life was ended by a man who was blind in a different way, blinded by prejudice," her brother would say later.

Just minutes after shooting LaManno, the attacker was handcuffed and loaded into the back seat of an Overland Park police cruiser. "My name is Glenn Miller. I'm an anti-Semite. I hate goddamn Jews," he declared to the officers. "How many'd I get?"

17

ABOUT TWO WEEKS BEFORE HE opened fire at the Jewish Community Center, Glenn Miller had driven himself to the emergency room in Aurora, Missouri. His breathing problem, he figured, was probably the long-term result of the cigarettes he'd smoked daily from the time he was sixteen until about five years earlier, when he quit cold turkey. He was proud of himself but knew he'd probably waited too long.

Miller insisted that he be admitted to the hospital, but the ER doctor refused, telling him "there wasn't much" they could do for his emphysema. What was most likely intended as a reassurance—that Miller could go home, that he was going to be fine—was taken by the patient as a dire warning. It was a sign, Miller was to explain later, that his death was imminent.

"I felt such an exhilaration overtake me, such joy. Like a ton had been lifted off of my shoulders, because I knew what I was going to do," Miller would recount. "Freedom. That's the word: freedom. I felt freedom for the first time in forty-eight years knowing that I was going to strike a blow for my people, a physical harm, violent blow for the preservation of my people and for the future for white children."

The first step was to get the guns, which, as a two-time felon he couldn't purchase for himself. He enlisted a friend named Mark— "kind of a semi-retarded fellow" according to Miller—to buy the guns at a local Walmart, telling him that they were gifts for his children. Next, Miller had to locate his target. He was paranoid, as he began searching the Internet, that federal agents might be monitoring his online activity. His fears were unfounded, though. Miller hadn't been a major player in the white supremacist movement and Far Right politics for years, and federal law enforcement had long since abandoned the type of large-scale monitoring of white supremacists it had undertaken in the 1990s. In his haste, Miller settled for the first potential target he came across: the Jewish Community Center in Kansas City, Kansas.

When he went on a scouting trip, Miller left the guns at home, assuming police would accost him. He drove right up to the JCC, even getting out of his car to walk around. No one stopped him. Not one police officer. He was dumbstruck.

So, Miller kept going back, making four or five visits to the center and making mental notes. Not only was the seventy-three-year-old's mobility limited but also even mild physical exertion left him winded. One afternoon, when Miller pulled off a country highway for some shooting practice, it took him nearly an hour just to climb out of his truck, load, and fire the guns. His ideal target, he concluded, would be an outside gathering—a rally or concert or communal meal—where he could just walk up and begin shooting. But, it seemed, such events never took place at the community center. He briefly considered another target—a local Jewish restaurant—but couldn't manage to locate it. Then he saw the flier for the KC SuperStar competition. People from all around the area would be coming to the JCC to perform in what he assumed must be an all-Jewish talent show.

But when the day arrived, Miller had second thoughts. He got to the center around noon and waited nearly forty-five minutes. He didn't see anyone in the parking lot. "There's nothing here," he thought. "You can't do anything today."

Miller began the drive home to Missouri but after just a few miles, his gut tugged at him. He pulled into a shopping center parking lot.

Was he really going to chicken out? Was he going to squander his final chance? What if he got pulled over on the way home? he thought. He had two shotguns, a .38-caliber revolver, and a .30-caliber carbine rifle with him in his white Suzuki Forenza. As a two-time felon, an arrest for gun possession would send him to prison for the rest of his life. No, Miller told himself, if he was going to risk dying in prison, he was at least going to do what he'd come here to do. "I got to thinking," Miller would recall, "'If you don't do it today, you might die and not get another chance.'"

And so he pulled back onto the interstate, turned around, and proceeded to the Jewish Community Center in Kansas City.

When, more than a year later, it came time to receive the wages of his sin, Miller could barely contain his excitement. "Frazier Glenn Miller Jr.," he declared when it was time to identify himself for the court reporter. (He also went by the names Glenn Miller and Frazier Glenn Cross.) "Bright-eyed and bushy tailed and chomping at the bit."

Johnson County district attorney Stephen Howe, the man charged with leading the prosecution, had been looking forward to taking his son to lunch and then to the pool on April 13, 2014, when he got a frantic phone call about the shooting and raced to the scene. Law enforcement determined relatively quickly that Miller had acted alone. But it would be reductive to think of him as a lone wolf. For most of his life, he'd bathed in the filthy waters of bigotry, drenched in dark ideologies that preached hatred and spite. "He is absolutely one of the most evil people I have ever been around," Howe would tell me years later.

Few of the facts were in dispute. As District Attorney Howe methodically set the scene in his opening argument, the attack began in the parking lot, where Miller executed Reat Underwood and his grandfather William Corporon before turning his fire on the building. He emptied his shotgun, littering the ground with green Remington shells, before switching to a rifle. Then he moved on to Village Shalom, a nearby Jewish retirement community, where he murdered Terri LaManno as she begged for her life in the parking lot. He confronted a second woman, demanding, "Are you a Jew?" When she insisted she wasn't, Miller allowed her to live and moved on. Ironically, he managed to carry out one of the deadliest anti-Semitic attacks in U.S. history without killing a single Jew—all three of his victims were Christians. But he didn't know that yet, so he drove to a nearby elementary school, parked, and celebrated by taking a few gulps from the fifth of Wild Turkey he'd brought along.

Even though Miller's guilt was clear, the trial still presented a challenge. He was defending himself, having fired his legal team. With a pro se defendant, prosecutors have to make sure not only to secure a conviction but also to make sure that the trial itself is fair—which is significantly harder when the accused refuses to employ professional defense attorneys. In thirty years of trying cases, Howe had never tried such a serious case in which the defendant represented himself, and, in researching the matter, his office found only a handful of similar cases in the entire country.

Miller had no interest in contesting the facts. He had done the things of which he stood accused. And he was proud of it. The trial, which stretched across several months, would not be a debate over his culpability. Instead, the aging Klansman hoped these legal proceedings would provide him the one thing he'd been denied for decades. He now had uncensored platform from which to proselytize about the alleged crisis he'd devoted his life to combating: a genocide of white Americans at the hands of blacks, immigrants, homosexuals, and, worst of all, Jews.

"We didn't feel that, because he was pro se, we could limit his testimony in any way," Howe explained to me, resulting in hours of Miller's spouting racist conspiracy theories in open court. "His right to present his case, despite him droning on for a long period of time about his twisted view of the world . . . we felt we had to let it happen."

"You have to understand what motivates me," Miller told the jurors as he began his testimony from the stand. "What's in my head? What made me do such a thing? What would make a seventy-three-year-old happily married man with six children and grandchildren living out on a nice farm in Missouri, a fairly nice house with a garden, cows—I raised French bulldog puppies. I always had a lot of them . . . I've just had a wonderful life . . ."

IN HIS CLASSIC 1954 BOOK *The Nature of Prejudice*, social psychologist Gordon Allport charts the progression of negative actions associated with prejudice: (1) antilocution (voicing those prejudices), (2) avoiding those against whom one is prejudiced, (3) actively discriminating against the group, (4) physical attacks, and (5) attempts at extermination. While the earlier stages consist of entirely legal, constitutionally protected behavior, they create the conditions that breed violence.

"Activity on one level makes transition to a more intense level easier," Allport explains. "It was Hitler's antilocution that led Germans to avoid their Jewish neighbors and erstwhile friends. This preparation made it easier to enact the Nuremberg Laws of discrimination, which, in turn, made the subsequent burning of synagogues and street attacks upon Jews seem natural. The final step in the macabre progression was the ovens at Auschwitz." When it comes to prejudice, "Violence is always an outgrowth of milder states of mind," Allport writes. "Most barking does not lead to biting, yet there is never a bite without previous barking."

Frazier Glenn Miller Jr. had been barking for a half century, spending decades within the American white supremacist movement, his life story tracing the peaks and valleys of an increasingly desperate and despondent movement. A leading researcher of extremism describes Miller as "one of the pioneers in the modern hate world." In *A White Man Speaks Out*, a rambling memoir of more than a hundred pages that he published online while in federal prison in the late 1980s, Miller details his bigoted ideologies and the journey that brought him to them.

During the summer of 1974, Miller's father gave him a copy of the *Thunderbolt*, the official newspaper of the National States' Rights Party, a white supremacist organization founded in the late 1950s in opposition to racial integration and the civil rights movement. "Within two minutes of browsing through this sixteen-page tabloid," Miller would recall in his self-published autobiography, "I knew I had found a home within the American White Movement."

Though he never pinpoints the exact moment he began to hold racist views, Miller outlines the racist conspiratorial ideology that would be the organizing principle of his life. He despised immigrants. He disliked blacks. But Miller held a special, intense hatred for Jews, who he believed, like generations of white supremacists before him, controlled the government and the media, were behind efforts at gun control, and were engaged in a centuries-long effort to exterminate the white race.

"What makes white supremacist worldviews more comprehensive and textured than a simple animus toward nonwhites is their addition of the Jew, the nefarious foe who seeks to upend the natural racial order," journalist Talia Lavin writes in *Culture Warlords: My Journey into the Dark Web of White Supremacy*, an examination of the dark corners of the white supremacist Internet. "The Jewish-led plot to dilute the white race is multifaceted, according to the contemporary far right, and presents itself not only as an attack on 'traditional' (i.e., heterosexual and stereotypically virile) masculinity, but also as a plot to deliberately shift demographics within the United States to dilute the white share of the population."

Miller called the NSRP's headquarters and a month later was attending meetings of the organization's North Carolina chapter.

But after about a year and a half, he grew disillusioned. He'd been handing out literature and going to meetings, and yet it seemed the group was stagnant—its members were all older white racists, with little promise of reaching a younger generation. By 1976, he'd joined the National Socialist Party of America, a Nazi group headquartered in Raleigh, North Carolina, but there too he felt frustrated. "No matter how much the average White American might agree with us, they just plain would not associate themselves with the swastika or with the word *Nazi*," Miller concluded. In 1980 he decided to launch his own group, the Carolina Knights of the Ku Klux Klan. After his failed stint as a Nazi, it was an obvious choice.

"The Klan was not alien to society or un-American. If it were, the problem would have been much simpler. Rather the Klan was typically American," writes historian Kenneth T. Jackson in his 1967 examination *The Ku Klux Klan in the City, 1915–1930.* "It prospered and grew to national power by capitalizing on forces already existent in American society: our readiness to ascribe all good or all evil to those religions, races, or economic philosophies with which we agree or disagree, and our tendency to profess the highest ideals while actually exhibiting the basest of prejudices."

While the organization's history is marred by violence, in Miller's telling, his goal remained proselytizing to his white brethren in order to attract the masses to his movement. And his plan, as has been the case for any number of white supremacist leaders in recent decades, was to utilize the media to do so.

First, Miller began publishing a racist newspaper like the one that had first drawn him into the movement. Then he began honing his public speaking abilities, first at small rallies at his house and later during appearances in the mainstream media. His first television appearance came on a local debate show called *Pro and Con.* The program had previously aired a segment debating whether the state needed a black political party. Miller called the station, NBC affiliate WRAL, and demanded equal time to debate the question of whether the state needed a *white* political party. TV appearances like these helped Miller find new would-be recruits, who called his organization each time it was mentioned on-air. That empowered his group to hold rallies and marches, prompting additional media coverage, which, in turn, aided in recruitment efforts. Miller and other members of his group sought public office, both locally and at the state level, not because they thought they could win but because the resulting media coverage would provide a forum to spread their racist and anti-Semitic views.

He'd write and mail letters to the editors of newspapers around the state, and if they were not run, he'd follow up to demand explanations for why they had not been published. "At first, many newspapers were reluctant to print my letters, and some downright refused to. So, I devoted considerable attention convincing them otherwise, by writing or calling editors or owners, and pleading the First Amendment," Miller recalled. When that didn't work, he'd threaten to hold a Klan protest outside the newspaper office or stage a publicity stunt. Miller had some of his members wear green berets and undergo paramilitary training—prompting fresh rounds of media coverage about how his group was training for a race war. Once, Miller threatened to bring five hundred armed Klansmen to Clayton, North Carolina—bringing media attention not just locally but also nationally after the Associated Press wire picked up the story. "I couldn't have raised 500 armed men if my life had depended on it," Miller confides in his book. "But I had achieved my objective of media attention, and, as usual, it resulted in new members and supporters."

But by the early 1980s, Miller, and his movement, would undergo a foundational shift in mission and the justification of deploying violence to attain it. "Throughout its history, the Klan has been a conservative, not a revolutionary, organization," writes historian David Chalmers, in *Hooded Americanism: The First Century of the Ku Klux Klan*. "By 1980, a major shift had taken place in the

Klan's historic role. As the Klansmen saw it, they were not so much fighting to protect white dominance in America as they were to regain it." This was an American Whitelash.

Miller was visited by a young man named Robert Jay Mathews, who had also spent much of his life traversing the white supremacist movement and sharpening his racist, anti-Semitic worldview. As a child, he had joined the John Birch Society, a virulently anti-Communist right-wing political group that trafficked in racism. Later, he dropped out of high school to start the Sons of Liberty, a right-wing militia. Miller, meanwhile, became a regular at the Aryan Nations compound in Idaho and joined the National Alliance, the neo-Nazi group founded by William Luther Pierce, the author of *The Turner Diaries*. Miller avidly read that book, in addition to *Which Way Western Man?*, a rambling treatise that argued for genetic inferiority of black people and other minorities and warned of a Jewish plot to destroy the white race. The book's author, white supremacist William Gayley Simpson, argues for expelling Jewish people, black people, and immigrants and the formation of a white ethnostate. "It can hardly be denied that the White man today is in a desperate plight," Simpson writes. "Catastrophe hangs over us."

By the time he visited Miller, Mathews had founded the Order, a white supremacist terror group that aimed to foment a race war and overthrow the American government. (It was Order member David Lane who would coin the "14 words.") As was the case of the fictional terrorists in *The Turner Diaries*, the Order launched a counterfeiting operation and committed bank robberies and armored truck heists to finance their operation. In June 1984, its members assassinated Alan Berg, an outspoken liberal Jewish talk-radio host in Denver. According to Miller, later that year Mathews gave him $75,000, which he used to begin stockpiling weapons and ammunition. Not long afterward, on December 8, the thirty-one-year-old Order founder was killed during a chaotic shootout with

FBI agents while barricaded in his home on picturesque Whidbey Island, north of Seattle.

Legal trouble would soon derail Miller's plans to join the race war. The Southern Poverty Law Center had sued his Klan group over its harassment of black residents in North Carolina. To settle the case, Miller agreed to disband the organization, only to relaunch it just one month later under a new name: the White Patriot Party. The SPLC took Miller back to court for violating the agreement, landing him in prison for six months. When his organization disbanded, a desperate Miller issued a "declaration of war" against the United States government, explicitly calling on fellow white supremacists to murder Jews, black people, and SPLC founder Morris Dees.

Following a ten-day manhunt and standoff with federal agents, Miller was arrested in April 1987 and ultimately cut a deal with prosecutors to testify against fellow white supremacist leaders in a 1988 sedition trial in Fort Smith, Arkansas. The defendants—including Aryan Nations' founder Richard Butler and movement leader Louis Beam—were all acquitted. In exchange for his cooperation, Miller was given just five years in prison, of which he'd serve three.

In the decades that followed, Miller would work to regain his footing in the movement he'd betrayed, becoming a regular on the racist message boards that replaced the tracts and mailers. And then, after four decades in the movement, facing what he erroneously believed was his impending death, Miller decided it was time to carry out the violence for which he'd spent almost his entire adulthood preparing.

His rationale, refined over decades in the movement, was the same cited later by attackers in Pittsburgh, Buffalo, El Paso, Texas, and Christchurch, New Zealand: the belief in a Jewish-run conspiracy to use immigration and miscegenation to bring about an end to the white race. Those shooters were largely radicalized online and wrote rambling manifestos citing the great replacement theory. Their beliefs, in the main, were no different from those held by Miller.

"I did everything possible for thirty-five years working legally within the system to bring about change," he would later tell the judge. "I had good moral reasons for doing what I did. I had good intentions in my heart, and I believe what I believe. . . . I'm going to prove to them that Jews are committing genocide against white people."

19

FOR MINDY CORPORON, THE DAYS and hours after the shooting that took the lives of her son and her father all flowed together in her memory. The hospital, the grieving, the vigils, the funeral plans. Throughout it all, she assumed it had all been some sort of accident, a mistake of some sort.

It wasn't until seven months later, when Miller gave a jailhouse interview to the *Kansas City Star*, that Corporon learned of the depths of his bigotry. The attacks, he told the reporter, were "for the specific purpose of killing Jews."

"Because of what I did, Jews feel less secure. . . . As for these . . . white people who are accomplices of the Jews, who attend their meetings and contribute to their fund-raising efforts and who empower the Jews, they are my enemy too. A lot of white people who associate with Jews, go to Jewish events, and support them know that they're not safe either, thanks to me."

By the time the full details of Miller's methodical planning and long-hardened ideology trickled out at the trial, Corporon had stopped tuning in. She avoided the courtroom, unsure if she'd be able to control her emotions. "I just didn't need any more pain," she explained.

The transcripts of the trial are difficult to follow. For days, Miller quibbled with rulings, ranted when he was given a chance to speak, and objected forcefully each time he was cut off. "He's not stupid,"

Howe told me. "He spent his entire time trying to bait the judge and my prosecution team to get us to create errors."

Just one sentence into Miller's opening statement, the jury had to clear the room so that Judge Thomas Kelly Ryan could explain to the defendant that he was not allowed to reveal the fact that there had been talks between him and prosecutors about a plea deal. Later in the trial, when Ryan asked him if he understood a motion brought by the prosecutor, Miller wisecracked, "Translate it into redneck."

"Pardon?" asked the judge.

"I'm just kiddin'. Just let it slide," Miller replied. "I'm in a good mood today, Judge."

As the trial drew to a close, the defendant had a request for the judge. Over the weekend, he'd spent hours typing up his closing statement. Now, on the day he had waited for, Miller wanted an opportunity to lay out why he did what he had done, to warn the white world that it needed to follow his example and enlist in the race war before it was too late. And, unlike earlier in the trial, where nearly every statement of his was cut off by an objecting prosecutor or a chiding judge, Miller hoped to deliver his final message as an uninterrupted soliloquy.

"You promised me the day would come when I would be able to have my day in court and speak my honest mind about everything—particularly about everything I was thinking on that day. So, I don't want these two clowns over there interrupting me and breaking the rhythm of my final statement." Miller gestured toward the prosecution bench. "I have a lot of hate in me, everybody knows that. And I want to express it."

But Judge Ryan was appropriately unconvinced. No, he told Miller, he would not bar the prosecution from leveling legal objections. After a brief argument—"You're a liar!" Miller shouted when the judge assured him that he'd received a fair trial—the jury was called in, and closing arguments began.

The prosecution was seeking the death penalty, and its argument was simple: Miller had deliberately targeted his three victims and put scores more in danger. He displayed no remorse; instead, he was bursting with pride. Howe said to me later that if this crime did not deserve the death penalty, then no crime does.

"He sat there on the stand and spoke with a smile on his face and chuckled and gleefully recalled what he did that day," Howe reminded the jury. "That is heinous, extremely wicked, and shockingly evil. And let's remember a quote he said on that one jail tape: 'Moments after killing these people, I've never felt such exhilaration, overpowering joy, total, absolute freedom.'"

While in many cases, a defendant's age and health, as well as his or her belief system, would be used by defense attorneys to argue for mercy, in this case, those were, in fact, the motivating force behind Miller's crimes. "Folks, you got to see firsthand during this trial what a hate crime looks like," Howe noted. "Its foundation is based on hate of others who are different than him."

Miller's ideology was a mixed media mosaic of radical and hyperbolic right-wing talking points constructed atop a foundation of racial hatred. He railed against the "Jew-controlled" media and its efforts to demand "tolerance." He disparaged blacks and gays, and decried abortions. Illegal immigration, he declared, was an invasion that threatened the nation's very existence.

"Tolerance, taught by the media, is, in reality, tyranny in disguise. The media bosses, the Jew media bosses, demand we tolerate that which threatens us and which inevitably will destroy our race in Western civilization." Today such a statement, with the possible exception of the explicit anti-Semitism, would not feel out of place as part of a Tucker Carlson monologue on Fox News. "When I attacked the Jewish Community Center," Miller went on, "I felt in my heart and soul that I was attacking our slave masters; members of the tribe that's committing genocide against our people."

Laid out so clearly, it was impossible to not see Miller's belief system—and the entire white supremacist ideology—for what it truly is: an unhinged conspiracy theory.

It went on like this for a half hour. And then, as he delivered his final words to the jury, a Nazi salute.

The jurors had heard his ideology, put up with weeks of his conspiracies and delusions. Now it was time for them to deliberate. Just two hours later they rendered their verdict: guilty. Ultimately, Frazier Glenn Miller Jr. was sentenced to death. As he was dragged out of the courtroom, the last words of his that made it into the official record were screams of "Death to the Jews!"

20

MINDY CORPORON WAS IN THE car with her husband and son Lucas, driving back to their new home in Florida after a Fourth of July vacation, when she decided she was finally ready to call the former white supremacist.

It had been four years since the shooting, but only now had she begun to really grapple with the evil that had visited her family. In the months afterward, Mindy had busied herself with ensuring that her slain loved ones would not be forgotten. She launched the Faith Always Wins Foundation, a community group that hosted an annual event called SevenDays: Make a Ripple, Change the World, in which local students take part in visual art, essay, and songwriting competitions, and are taught the values of unity and community service. Her program was seen locally as a massive success, and her story one of a woman who'd been visited by evil yet pushed forward for good.

One of her admirers is Prosecutor Howe. Glenn Miller's goal, he told me, "was to get people to believe in his beliefs, but all he did was galvanize the community to support people from different walks of life. Mindy talks about how we're all equal in the eyes of God. We may look or act different or have different religious beliefs. Our community bonded together with her leadership. As horrific as this thing was," he said, "something positive came from it."

But up until then, Mindy had avoided any further exploration of white supremacy itself. It was easier, more comfortable, to look away. "I think that we avoid pain when we're not ready for it," she'd say to me later. "I wasn't sure that I wanted to know more. I wasn't sure that I was ready or healthy enough."

Then, in May 2018, she began receiving what she believed were unmistakable signs. On three separate occasions, someone sent her a link to the story of a reformed white supremacist. First, she read the book *Autobiography of a Recovering Skinhead: The Frank Meeink Story,* by a former neo-Nazi who left the movement after a stretch in prison. Next, she listened to an interview with Derek Black, whose father had founded the white supremacist online forum Stormfront and whose godfather was the notorious Klansman David Duke. Although he'd been raised in the white supremacist movement, Black would go on to publicly renounce his prior views and the movement. Finally, she listened to a TED Talk given by Christian Picciolini, in which the former white supremacist explained for thirteen minutes how he'd fallen into a lifestyle of hate but eventually pulled himself out.

She reached out to all three of them. Picciolini was the only one who responded. He told Mindy that he knew about the shooting that had killed her father and son, and that he remembered Miller from his days in the movement. He offered to help her any way that he could. She responded that she didn't know if there was any way he could help her, or if she even wanted to talk to him, but that she appreciated the work he was doing.

Two months later, she had read his book, *White American Youth,* and decided that she was ready to talk. Tears welled in Mindy's eyes before she'd even finished dialing his number. Was this the right thing to do? Or was she betraying her own son and father?

But within minutes, her hesitations melted away. Picciolini was caring and gentle. The most important thing, he told her, was talking to survivors like herself.

"I remember being so, kind of, humbled, by the fact that she had approached me," Picciolini told me later. "She wanted answers. She wanted to know why. She couldn't understand what had happened to her son or her father. She'd spent years trying to figure out how could people do something like that."

Picciolini started out in the movement in 1987, when he was just fourteen, and stayed in for about a decade until his midtwenties. He'd attended rallies and meetings with Glenn Miller and remembered the firebrand newsletters he'd circulate. But even as Miller was among the most outspoken, he didn't really stick out. Everyone was a self-styled racist revolutionary. They were preparing for the race war—even if most of them were more talk than action.

"Hate is a really complicated thing," Picciolini told me later. "It wasn't that somebody hated their loved ones. The perpetrator didn't even know the victims. It so often stems from self-hatred being projected onto other people. . . . What that person had was self-hatred and was a coward who didn't know how to deal with it."

Mindy floated the idea of Picciolini coming to Kansas City to speak at an event for her nonprofit. When they hung up after an hour, Mindy's son Lucas declared that she was so brave for having had the conversation. But part of her still wasn't so sure. She had to know for certain that putting Picciolini onstage was the right decision. So, she flew to Naples, Florida, to meet with him ahead of the event.

"He's burly, and tattoos all over," she described him to me later. "He's this brick of a man. But he's gentle and kind and gave me a big hug."

Almost a year of trading emails and phone calls had passed before Corporon and Picciolini finally shared a stage, headlining the annual SevenDays event. Along with Picciolini, Mindy hosted a conversation with a woman named Shannon Foley Martinez, another former white supremacist. The audience that night was almost twice as large as had been expected. Mindy swallowed her nerves. She had never conducted a live onstage interview before. By now, she had spent years dealing with the aftermath of hatred. Now, Mindy told her audience, she wanted to know why it had happened in the first place.

"That's what I'm searching for," she said to the eight hundred people who crammed into Kansas City's United Methodist Church of the Resurrection. "And that's what I'm finding out."

At the time of the event, Christian Picciolini and Martinez were perhaps America's two most famous former skinheads.

Picciolini has spent years telling his story, in a TED Talk that's been viewed more than four million times, multiple National Public Radio segments, two autobiographical books, and in a sit-down with Scott Pelley on *60 Minutes*.

As the child of Italian immigrants, he was bullied severely in the Chicago suburb where he was raised. Picciolini's life changed forever due to a chance encounter with Clark Martell, the founder of the city's most notorious and violent skinhead group. Martell had spotted the fourteen-year-old smoking a joint and chided him, "That's what the Communists and the Jews want you to do, to keep you docile." Before long, Picciolini had been sucked into the movement, listening to racist punk rock and spending the hours his parents were at work with a cadre of neo-Nazi skinheads.

Two years later, Martell was sent to prison for beating up a woman who had quit the movement and who allegedly had black friends. He'd then used her blood to draw a swastika on the wall of her home. That put Picciolini in line to succeed him as gang leader. He was sixteen. It would take years before he found his way out.

While Picciolini embraced the movement in search of love, Martinez found it while searching for a platform on which to express her rage. At fourteen, she'd been sexually assaulted at a party. The teenager began listening to darker music and seeking out darker crowds. She went from skateboarders, to punks, and then to skinheads. In the years to come, she'd drift deeper and deeper into the darkness, attending Klan rallies and paramilitary trainings in order to prepare for the pending race war. "I only hung out with other white supremacists and other white nationalists and white power people," Martinez explained in 2019. It was only after she began living with the mother of one of her boyfriends, whose household provided stability and who encouraged her to go to college, that she left the movement.

Today Picciolini and Martinez work to pull others out of the white supremacist movement, a grueling task that often involves hours of back-and-forths and debates with self-proclaimed fascists. Among at least some anti-racism activists, there is a strand of skepticism regarding well-branded former Nazis such as Picciolini and Martinez. It's not so much that they doubt the reformed racists' motives or sincerity but more . . . *distaste* at how the narratives of their transformations are deployed in the national conversation. The fear, not unfounded, is that an emphasis on redemption and reconciliation can mute the depths of the darkness from which they've emerged and the seriousness with which it must be taken.

As I read over a partial transcript of the Kansas City event, I was struck by a set of remarks made by Martinez in response to an audience member who asked her what role the federal government and the media could play in further deradicalizing the population. Often such questions prompt niceties about forgiveness and listening and appeals to compassion and "shared humanity." Yet Martinez, who just moments earlier had spoken movingly about the importance, when attempting to pull someone out of extremism, of truly listening to them, made it clear to the audience that the problem goes deeper than "dialogue" or interpersonal "forgiveness."

"If we are serious about dismantling white supremacy, we are going to have to have some incredibly difficult, soul-searching conversations, and we have to acknowledge that white supremacy is an inherent part of the history of our country," she said, adding, "We can't get to a part of the apology where we are making meaningful amends if we do not first acknowledge the harm that we have done."

For what it's worth, I wrote letters to Glenn Miller in prison to request an interview and attempted to broker access to him via officials at Kansas's maximum-security El Dorado Correctional Facility, where he'd been incarcerated. But I was never able to reach him. Similarly, calls and emails to his children and wife went unanswered. I don't know that these pages are missing much, though, by his lack of participation. Throughout his life, Miller made clear the content of his heart and the aims of his actions.

Led off to await his death sentence, Miller vowed to work on another book. But once he was sentenced, he faded into obscurity. Because he was being held on death row, the vast majority of his time was spent alone, with no cellmates to indoctrinate or rant to. "We neutered his ability to be able to spread his venom," Steve Howe told me. "When he was shipped off to the penitentiary, we never heard from him again."

"I feel sorry for him," Mindy told me nearly six years after the shooting, in early 2020. "I feel like that if you have that much hate, it's because you don't know how to love. And if you don't know how to love, it's because no one has loved you."

Mindy was even considering visiting Miller. Sometimes she would envision what the meeting would be like, picturing herself driving to the prison where he sat awaiting execution. Maybe she'd speak to him through a Plexiglas partition by one of those direct-connect telephones. Or perhaps she would be led to a visitation room and be seated across the table from him. Either way, she knew what she would say. On behalf of her slain father and son, she'd look Miller in the eye and tell him, "You didn't win."

As it turned out, she never got the chance. In May 2021, prison officials announced that Glenn Miller had died in prison of natural causes at the age of eighty.

PART V

A MOVEMENT RISES

If there is no struggle, there is no progress. Those who profess to favor freedom, and yet depreciate agitation, are men who want crops without plowing up the ground. They want rain without thunder and lightning. They want the ocean without the awful roar of its many waters. This struggle may be a moral one; or it may be a physical one; or it may be both moral and physical; but it must be a struggle. Power concedes nothing without a demand.

—FREDERICK DOUGLASS, ABOLITIONIST, 1857

21

THE BIRTHDAY GIRL COULDN'T HAVE worn a wider smile on New Year's Eve 2008 as a crowd of family and friends packed into her mother's house for a celebration, complete with seafood gumbo and carrot cake.

Earlier in the day, Wanda Johnson had gotten a call from her twenty-two-year-old son, Oscar, who wanted to know if she wanted anything special for the gathering. Her request was simple: a couple of crabs and some shrimp. That afternoon, Oscar swung by Farmer Joe's supermarket and picked up a sailor's haul.

It was no surprise that Oscar had come through. If there was one thing Wanda knew about her son, it was that he was always looking to help. One time, when he was a boy, she caught him running an extension cord out through the back door of their house. Confronted by his mother, Oscar explained that he was lending power to an impoverished family that lived downstairs so that they could keep their refrigerator running. She laughed and forgave him for the skyrocketing electricity bill. What else should she expect from the son who volunteered as an usher and sang in the choir at Palma Ceia Baptist Church in their hometown of Hayward, California? When a stroke left her aging father without the use of the left side of his body, Oscar sprung into a caretaker role, so attentive that the family began addressing him as "Grandpa's left hand."

It's not that there hadn't been stumbles in a life whose circumstances were calibrated for difficulty. Wanda had raised Oscar as a single mother, his father having been sentenced to life in prison before the boy was even born. (He served thirty years for a murder he insisted he did not commit.) Oscar himself had been arrested five times, at least once for dealing drugs, and spent close to two months in county jail.

In his midteens, Oscar had started cutting classes and eventually dropped out of school in the tenth grade, not long after meeting Sophina Mesa, the girlfriend who would give birth to his daughter, Tatiana, and eventually become his fiancée. He ended up in the county jail for a time, after running from a traffic stop and being found with a gun. Those months had been hard on them all. Now that Oscar was out, struggling to find and hold down enough work to support his young family, Wanda was feeling particularly protective. He was a grown man, but he was still her son. It was her job to keep him safe.

Oscar's plan that night was to head into San Francisco to watch the ball drop with some friends. Nothing too crazy, he assured his skeptical mother. But still Wanda had questions. How were they getting there? Are they sure they wanted to drive? Oscar didn't drink and insisted it wouldn't be a big deal for him to man the wheel. Still, his mother urged, wouldn't it make more sense for the group to take the train into the city?

Wanda Johnson carried the burden of being the mother of a black son. She still remembered when Oscar began growing facial hair in the eighth grade, and how often he'd be stopped by the police on his bike ride home from school. Sometimes they'd let him go. Other times they'd handcuff him and give him a ticket for not wearing a bicycle helmet. Now he was older, bigger, and likely to be seen as more of a threat. "I worried about him all of the time," she would later tell me.

And so, on the final evening of his life, at his mother's urging,

Oscar Grant boarded the BART train to San Francisco. That seemingly small decision would set in motion a series of events that ultimately led to the largest American civil rights movement in decades.

Wanda tried to stay awake that night, watching television with a friend, but drifted to sleep in her chair. Then a frantic call from Oscar's girlfriend jolted her awake. It was difficult to make out the words, and even harder to make sense of them. Oscar had been shot. She needed to get to Highland Hospital in Oakland.

Around two in the morning, on the train ride back across San Francisco Bay, Oscar and his friends had gotten into a scuffle with another group of riders. Police arrived, after having been told that a group of black males, wearing all black, had been involved in the fight. What exactly happened next would be highly contested for years until, in 2019, the results of the Bay Area Rapid Transit's internal affairs report was finally made public.

The cops pulled Oscar and his friends off the train and lined them up on the platform at Fruitvale Station. Amid the chaos, bystanders pulled out their cell phones and began recording. Witnesses heard officers telling Oscar and his friends to "shut the fuck up," and one officer, Anthony Pirone, grew incensed that Grant was filming on his cell phone. As Pirone roughly pinned Grant to the ground, another officer, Johannes Mehserle, joined the fray. Grant was sprawled facedown on the floor when Mehserle pulled out his service weapon and fired a bullet into his back.

By the time Wanda arrived at the hospital, a gaggle of friends and loved ones were already there. She ordered them to be quiet, demanding they all bow their heads and grasp hands in a prayer. Soon Wanda had fled to the hospital's chapel, where she silently offered a mother's desperate plea on behalf of her son. She asked God to save him. She asked that He touch the hands of the doctors and nurses in the operating room. She prayed that the blood would clot, and that Oscar would be granted the breath of life.

But there was nothing she or the emergency room doctors could do. The bullet had pierced Oscar's lung and ricocheted devastatingly through his insides. Hospital workers had gotten him breathing off of a machine, but, despite attempts at transfusions, couldn't get the blood to clot. When she was finally let into the room, Wanda stroked her son's head; she tried to talk him out of dying. Then, tears dripping from her cheeks, Wanda walked out of the operating room to tell the others.

22

THE DEATH OF OSCAR GRANT, just a month and a half after Barack Obama's election and three weeks before the forty-fourth president's inauguration, would be just the first in an unrelenting series of killings by police of black men and women across the country, prompting the largest sustained American protest movement since the civil rights era. Millions would pour into the streets to chant the names—Eric Garner, Michael Brown, Sandra Bland, Philando Castile, Breonna Taylor, George Floyd—and demand justice. The cause was as old as the nation itself: the failure of the police to provide safety and justice for black Americans and the indignities that black communities faced from those sworn to serve and protect. But this new era, in which such encounters could be captured on cell phone cameras and then instantaneously published on social media for the world to see, forced white Americans, and others around the world, to see the experiences that generations of black Americans had testified to but that the nation had refused to acknowledge.

Before long, the bystander videos showing Oscar's final moments on the platform of Fruitvale Station had been posted online and were playing on a loop on the local news. Protests and riots broke out. Clergy petitioned the local prosecutor, demanding that charges be filed.

"If it had not been for the community protesting and insisting that the officer be charged, the officer probably would have never got charged," Wanda Johnson would tell me later. "It was the community that really stood with us. What made Oscar's case unique is that it was the first time that cell phones could actually film it."

Ryan Coogler, then a film student, was home in the Bay Area for the holidays. "When I saw the footage on the news and online, I was immediately emotionally moved and shocked," he said in 2013. "I realized that Oscar could have been me. We were the same age, his friends looked like my friends, and we wore the same type of clothes." News coverage of the case left him heartbroken. "During the trial," he recalled, "I saw how the situation became politicized. Oscar was either seen as a saint, or he was seen as a monster, who got what he deserved that night depending on which side of the fence people stood on. I felt that in that process, Oscar's truth was lost."

Coogler began writing a script. Before long, Wanda heard from Academy Award–winning actor Forest Whitaker, who had signed on to produce Coogler's script. At first, she was hesitant. Wanda knew that once she signed on, the end product would be out of her hands and in the control of actors and producers and directors. But she agreed to explore the process, and soon a procession was making its way through Oakland. Coogler, set to make his directorial debut, sat with her in her mother's living room, where the family had spent Oscar's final night. Next came actor Michael B. Jordan, who had been cast to play Oscar. Then came Octavia Spencer, who was charged with portraying Wanda herself. She felt comforted by the care each took to understand not just Oscar's life but also his death. And the resulting film, *Fruitvale Station*, an intimate portrait of Oscar's final day, was an immediate hit upon its release in 2013.

The years to follow would see the rise of what is widely known as the Black Lives Matter movement (referred to, by activists, as the Movement for Black Lives), a societal and political force that has upended American institutions and continues to press for fundamental changes to the criminal legal system. Yet this movement for justice, itself a response to the white supremacy still embedded in our nation's structures and systems, would soon prompt yet another round of American backlash.

23

IN 2019, A DECADE SINCE Oscar Grant's death, I traveled to Ferguson, Missouri, to reconnect with a crucial witness to another pivotal police shooting.

By 2014, the spark ignited by Grant's death had become a nationally burning flame. The years since had brought the killing of Trayvon Martin, an unarmed black teenager gunned down by a community watchman named George Zimmerman in Sanford, Florida, in 2012. Ryan Coogler's *Fruitvale Station* debuted in movie theaters on July 12, 2013. The very next day, a jury acquitted Zimmerman of murder charges. The frustration simmering in the hearts of black Americans was ready to boil over. Now a new year had brought the videotaped death of Eric Garner, asphyxiated by a policeman's illegal choke hold. He too was unarmed. Then, just three weeks later, on a sunny summer Saturday, Officer Darren Wilson shot and killed Michael Brown in Ferguson. No weapon was found on the teenager, whose body was left in the street for hours. Protests raged for months.

Yet, in the five years since Brown's death, the man he was with that day, Dorian Johnson, had become a ghost, fading from both headlines and minds. I don't know how long it had been since I'd thought of him. But as I sat to be interviewed about my reporting on Ferguson for a documentary pegged to the five-year anniversary, a producer asked me if I knew what had happened to Johnson. When I realized that I didn't, I knew I needed to find him.

Johnson, twenty-two at the time, hadn't been interviewed in years. But I was eventually able to track down a Saint Louis record label for which he had recorded some rap music. Before long, I was standing on Canfield Drive, the street where Brown was killed, as Johnson walked me back through the events of that day.

The shooting shook Johnson deeply. Even as we spoke, years later, he still choked up while discussing the details. No matter how hard he tried, he could never erase the image from his mind, playing in a haunting loop, of the moment Brown's soul left his body.

It was cruelly fitting that Johnson would end up playing a starring role in perhaps the most controversial police shooting in the nation's history. Like many young men from his neighborhood, a depressing stretch of Saint Louis dotted with liquor stores and abandoned properties, he'd been stalked all his life by violence and trauma. Johnson's left eye is discolored from a pencil that pierced his cornea, thrown by a classmate on the first day of seventh grade. His high school football career was cut short when he was struck in the knee by a stray bullet on the way home from practice his junior year. Two years later, in 2009, his best friend was killed in a drive-by shooting. A year after that, his younger brother was killed after losing control of his Pontiac Grand Am. Johnson raced to the scene, only to be handcuffed by police and thrown in the back of a police van. Year after year, he had been dealt bad hands.

But by 2014, it seemed his luck was changing. That spring, he'd managed to move with his longtime girlfriend and their newborn daughter out of the city and into a third-floor walk-up near the back of the Canfield Green apartment complex. For a man who'd spent his entire life in the rough Walnut Park neighborhood of North Saint Louis, relocating to the suburb of Ferguson, tucked between the airport and downtown, just north of the city, was a big step up.

Johnson had made it a habit of inviting guys from his new neighborhood into the apartment to listen to music and play video games, and it was during one of these impromptu hangouts that he met "Big Mike" Brown. Despite the four-year age difference—Brown was eighteen and had just finished a summer program to secure his high school degree—the two hit it off discussing their love of music and Brown's newfound exploration of Christianity. Johnson could tell that Mike was looking for someone to talk to. But their only other substantive conversation came on August 9, the day of the shooting.

Brown showed up at Dorian's apartment at two in the morning, wanting to talk. His grandmother and stepmother were both sick, he said, and he'd had a premonition that he could heal them through prayer. But his friends and family wouldn't listen. The previous afternoon, in what would be their final conversation, Brown's father hung up on him.

Johnson went inside to get dressed but fell asleep instead. When he woke up hours later, he ran into Brown in the apartment complex parking lot. He apologized for having blown him off and offered to continue the conversation. Within minutes, the two were walking up the street toward Ferguson Market & Liquor.

According to Johnson, Brown was convinced that he was in the midst of a spiritual epiphany and that strange things were happening all around him. He was behaving erratically and making grandiose pronouncements, saying, for instance, that he was destined to change the world.

The pair entered the market. Earlier that day, Brown had tried unsuccessfully to barter with a clerk, offering a baggie of marijuana in exchange for a soda and two boxes of cigarillos. Now Brown looked at a different clerk. "Do you know who I am?" He added quickly, "You know who I am." Then, surveillance video shows, Brown reached across the counter, grabbed the cigarillos, and shoved the clerk. He handed some of the stolen cigarillos to Johnson and lumbered toward the exit. Stunned by what had just happened, Johnson set the stolen cigars down on the counter and followed Mike out the door.

The duo had made it a few blocks down West Florissant Avenue, one of Ferguson's major arteries, and turned down Canfield Drive, just a few hundred feet from Johnson's front door, when they were confronted by a Ferguson cop. Darren Wilson would later tell prosecutors that he'd driven his police SUV past Brown and Johnson, realized the pair fit the description of the two young men who'd just robbed the market, and then quickly doubled back. Moments later, gunshots rang out.

24

EACH TIME I INTERVIEW THE mother of someone who has been killed by the police, I can't help but wonder about the moment—*that* moment—when her worst nightmare became reality. Wanda Johnson had been blissfully asleep on a living room chair when she got the call about Oscar. Gwen Carr had been on a break from her job as an MTA train operator when her phone suddenly lit up with text messages about the police, untaxed cigarettes, and her son, Eric Garner. Lezley McSpadden was working her shift at a Saint Louis grocery store when she got the phone call that Michael Brown, the son she'd given birth to at the age of fifteen, had been shot by a police officer.

"I was disconnected from myself," McSpadden recalled. "And the only thing I remember is receiving the phone call. Hearing my sister—she was crying before she could even get it out. And when you have children, you feel somethin'. Even when they just fall and hurt themselves, you feel somethin'. And I felt something in my chest, in my gut. And that let me know my son had been hurt."

Her son's body was still lying on Canfield Drive, with crowds congregating at the police tape, when McSpadden and the rest of the family gathered in the kitchen of a nearby apartment. They'd never met Dorian Johnson before, and now they wanted to know what in the world had happened. Johnson was the eyewitness, and now he would feel the weight of the role.

Through thick tears, Johnson recounted how he and Brown had encountered a Ferguson policeman who yelled at them to stop walking in the street. Then the officer whipped around his SUV, grabbed Brown by the collar, and began struggling with the six-foot-four youth through the car window. A gunshot rang out, and Brown and Johnson dashed off in different directions. Dorian, having ducked behind a nearby parked car, watched as the officer pumped a half dozen bullets into Brown's body.

When Johnson finished, Brown's family had one request: tell the media. And so, minutes later, a trembling Johnson was staring into a local TV news camera, spitting out the words that would change both his life and the nation.

"He put his hands in the air," Johnson said of Brown in his final moments. "He started to get down, but the officer still approached with his weapon drawn. And he fired several more shots. And my friend died." Johnson's assertion that Brown was trying to surrender when Wilson killed him spawned a powerful rallying cry, chanted at protests across the country: "Hands up, don't shoot!"

Brown "stopped to turn around with his hands in the air and started to tell the officer that he was unarmed," Johnson said on MSNBC a few days after the shooting. "Before he can get his last words out, the officer fired several more shots."

Controversy over Johnson's account raged for months. The media that had descended on Ferguson knocked on doors, followed leads to find new witnesses, and searched—in vain—for any video that might have existed of the shooting. Several citizens came forward with accounts that matched Johnson's recollection. But Officer Wilson provided a starkly different version of the events of August 9, 2014.

According to him, Brown punched him through the driver's side window and later charged him on the street, forcing Wilson to shoot. Unbeknownst to the public was the fact that other witnesses had spoken, or would soon speak, to law enforcement and given accounts supporting the officer, suggesting that Brown had been moving toward Wilson, even charging at him, in the seconds before the shooting. Regrettably, all the confusion surrounding the case was exacerbated by the Ferguson Police Department, which remained frustratingly tight-lipped about what had happened that day. Other local authorities followed suit. More than a week passed before police identified Darren Wilson as the officer who had pulled the trigger, as well as made public any information about the liquor store robbery.

"His hands were definitely up when he turned around," Johnson told me when we spoke five years later, sticking to his story. "Whether his hands were up, or halfway up, or fully down or up, he was killed, and he was unarmed. He wasn't posing a threat."

Thousands poured into the streets, first from Ferguson and the surrounding communities and later from across the country. The demands were simple: they wanted the officer charged with a crime for killing Brown, they wanted an independent prosecutor, and they wanted sweeping changes to policing that would put an end to tragedies such as this. The demonstrations added to the momentum already building in New York, where protesters and activists continued to demand justice for Eric Garner. Soon, as more videos spread online, there were protests across America. In October thousands descended on Ferguson for a Freedom Rides–inspired pilgrimage organized by the founders of a relatively new activist organization called Black Lives Matter. By then, the young street protesters had begun launching their own activist groups. Clearly this was more than a fleeting moment.

And like the white supremacist movement whose ideology this new energy had emerged in part to combat, the black activists carried a mix of ideologies and backgrounds as they pressed for shared aims. Same religion, different denominations. There were longtime community organizers and clergy who had spent decades toiling to combat violence and poverty marching next to twenty-something men and women who'd previously been politically apathetic.

Yet as the weeks turned into months, it became increasingly clear that Officer Wilson would not face criminal charges. The prosecutor overseeing the case had rarely, if ever, charged police officers in connection to on-duty shootings. (My then-colleagues at the *Washington Post* would later document how rare such charges are nationwide: it almost never happens.) The Obama administration dispatched its top law enforcement official, Attorney General Eric Holder, to Ferguson; he launched his own investigations into both the shooting itself and the general practices of the Ferguson police.

The federal report on the investigation stated that several credible witnesses "gave varying accounts of exactly what Brown was doing with his hands"—including balling them up, holding them out, or pulling up his pants—"they all establish that Brown was moving toward Wilson when Wilson shot him," the federal report on the investigation concluded. That November, prosecutors declined to charge Wilson with a crime, touching off a fresh round of rioting.

By then, Johnson had become a ghost. He watched Ferguson burn from a Saint Louis hotel room. For weeks, his grandfather had been shuffling him from hotel to hotel, hiding him from a scoop-hungry press. Several conservative pundits were saying Johnson should be charged with perjury for lying to police about the shooting—a charge that would not, in fact, have been legally applicable. The young man, like many of the witnesses, officials, and journalists closest to the case, became the target of death threats. Each time Johnson opened his social media accounts, he found new threats. Every time he turned on the television, someone new was calling him a liar.

Within months, he had lost both his job cleaning train platforms and his new apartment in Ferguson. He was back in the city, sleeping on his mother's couch, his baby girl nestled on his chest.

The enduring celebrity was a torment. Strangers approached Johnson constantly—some to thank him for speaking up; others chewed him out. He couldn't hold down a job. While working maintenance at a nearby state park, Dorian noticed a vehicle that kept showing up during his shifts. Worried that he was being followed, he quit. He lost another job, as a line chef, after a customer recognized him and created a commotion.

Happily, by the time we met up in 2019, Johnson and his family had moved back to Ferguson, settling into a small house on a quiet side street. It is located just a few blocks from the police station, where demonstrators still gather on the anniversary of Mike Brown's death.

We walked along Canfield Drive that afternoon, with Johnson pointing out familiar spots. There's where Wilson stopped them. Here's where Johnson hid behind a car during the shooting. That's where Brown's body lay on the concrete.

With the sun setting behind us, he knelt and placed a hand on a plaque commemorating Brown's death. Big Mike was right, Johnson told me as we sat beneath a nearby tree. His death had changed the world.

25

SHAWN WASHINGTON, EXHAUSTED AFTER A long day on the road and a few hours spent gambling at a nearby casino, coasted his eighteen-wheeler onto the shoulder of the highway near a Saint Louis truck stop on December 5, 2018. He cranked up his favorite jazz station and drifted into the slumber that would soon upend his entire life.

The black forty-six-year-old slept most of the following day, and so his trucking company, concerned that he'd yet to deliver his trailer full of protein drinks to Indianapolis, started calling. When he didn't answer, and with the truck's GPS indicating that he was still in Saint Louis, the company phoned local police.

The first thing Washington remembers hearing were the heavy thuds as the officers' fists struck the side of his semi, echoing loud enough to jolt him awake. Washington's story is that he pulled on some pants and climbed to the front seat as the police screamed at him to get out of the vehicle. Their guns were drawn. Washington reached for his phone to record them. Then the passenger-side window shattered.

According to the St. Louis Metropolitan Police Department, it was an officer's fist that broke the window. But Washington assumed that the cops had opened fire. He dove into the driver's seat and sped off. It was a short chase, ending a few miles later when the semi crashed into a traffic pole. Then, Washington says, officers climbed into the truck. After macing him, punching him, and kicking him, they dragged his body from the rig. The next thing he remembers is riding in the back of an ambulance, simply glad to be alive.

The officers' official accounts told an entirely different story. They said a trucking company employee had told them Washington was likely inside the truck with a sex worker, and that when they heard movement inside, they set spike strips behind its tires and screamed for him to get out. Then, suddenly, the officers wrote, Washington put the truck in gear and drove off. After the truck crashed a few blocks later, the officers claimed that they found the driver with his fists clenched and held up in front of his face in a boxer's stance.

Washington was charged with felony resisting arrest, reckless driving, and damaging city property, as well as committing a crime with the use of a deadly weapon—namely, the semi. Even under the most favorable circumstances, a conviction or plea deal was going to cost him at least three years behind bars.

"I wanted it all to just go away," Washington told me the first time we spoke. Although he'd gotten into some trouble with the law as a teen, it had been decades since he'd faced any criminal charges. "I hoped it would be resolved; that we would be able to get it all straightened out."

After four days in the hospital, Washington was shipped to the St. Louis Medium Security Institution, commonly known as the Workhouse. Battered, sore, and still facing felonies, Washington thought he'd made it through hell. But his time there was just beginning.

It had been five years since the police shooting of Michael Brown, and the movement spawned by his death was still raging across the country. The city of Saint Louis remained among the most crucial battlegrounds upon which the fight over the future of the criminal legal system was being waged.

Kayla Reed is a Saint Louis activist who'd joined the Ferguson protests. "We tell a story of what happens after an uprising," she said. "In order for things to change, they don't really happen in the exact moment that the uprising is occurring. Not always. . . . If we're planting the seeds of change in people's minds, we have to kind of work the soil over a few years in a row to get some of those seeds to bear fruit—to actually be the policy changes and the cultural shifts and the transformation that we actually need to see in our communities." In the early days of the Ferguson protests, she used to hand out bottles of water and masks to help protesters withstand tear gas. In the ensuing years, she became one of the city's most consequential activists.

The years following Ferguson saw a wave of change brought about by sustained activism. Thousands of police departments reviewed their use-of-force policies and implemented body camera programs. A series of states, and some departments themselves, began publishing crucial law enforcement data that shed new light on killings by the police and incidents of alleged brutality. In response to a database project I helped launch at the *Washington Post* and a similar effort undertaken by the *Guardian*, the FBI announced that it would collect and release national data on police killings. (That promise was effectively abandoned following the election of Donald Trump.)

Activist groups such as Color of Change, an influential civil rights organization born during the digital era, redoubled their efforts to challenge the way black Americans are portrayed in the mainstream media, campaigning for the cancelation of television shows such as *COPS*, which, they argued, too often propagate dangerous stereotypes about racial minorities. Across the country, a wave of so-called progressive prosecutors swept into office, vowing to cease the prosecution and enforcement of heavy sentences for low-level crimes and to use their powers to investigate and prosecute problem police officers. Prosecutors play the most powerful role in the criminal legal system; within a handful of years, the prosecutors' offices in Chicago, Philadelphia, San Francisco, and Boston were among those run by dedicated reformers.

"A lot of people have always realized that we have not been treated fairly. It's just more obvious now, with all of the surveillance cameras and with camera phones. People are more aware. It's just more obvious now," Sybrina Fulton, Trayvon Martin's mother, told me in 2017, five years after his death. "And so now you have police officers that are being charged, officers that are going before a grand jury—those things didn't happen before, and now they're happening. It's definitely a move, it's just a slow move. It's almost like a turtle's move."

The change was certainly being felt in Ferguson. The city brought in a black police chief and elected its first black mayor. In 2020 Cori Bush, who had been a protester, unseated a longtime incumbent and was elected to Congress to represent the district that includes Ferguson. By then, both St. Louis County and the city had elected progressive prosecutors of their own. Next, local activists settled on a new, ambitious aim: closing the Workhouse.

The city's original Workhouse was constructed downtown in 1843 as a labor camp where prisoners could pay off criminal fines by crushing limestone for the city streets. The 1,200-bed facility, built in 1966, sits next to the Mississippi River, about seven miles north of the iconic Gateway Arch. For nearly as long as its four nondescript brick buildings have stood, the people housed there have complained about the prison's conditions, over which the city has been sued repeatedly.

Shawn Washington spent his first four days at the Workhouse in lockdown, housed twenty-four hours a day in a walk-in-closet-sized cell containing a bunk bed, a sink, a toilet, and a standoffish cellmate. Then he was moved to the general population, where dozens of men shared bunk beds in a single crowded room. It was the dead of winter, and most of the time the Workhouse was freezing. In calls from the jailhouse phone, Washington pleaded with family members to send him thermal pajamas. On the rare days when the heat worked, it was cranked so high that the inmates could barely breathe. The sleeping quarters and the kitchen, where Washington was given a job preparing food, were crawling with cockroaches and dotted with mice droppings. The entire place smelled like a putrid mix of mold and raw eggs.

For years, city officials argued that the conditions inside the Workhouse were not as inhumane as inmates alleged. "The only reason the narrative about conditions in the Workhouse persists is because people refuse to visit and see for themselves," Jimmie Edwards, the city's public safety director, told the *Guardian* newspaper in September 2018. Still, city officials took steps to reduce the number of people being held there.

The facility wasn't designed for long-term confinement but primarily for pretrial detainees. Activists note, though, that detention can last weeks or even months for suspects unable to afford bail. For Washington, his time at the Workhouse stretched nearly ninety days.

26

WHEN SOMEONE IS ARRESTED AND charged with a crime, he or she is treated one of three ways: deemed dangerous to the public and therefore detained until trial; freed based only on the promise of showing up at trial; or released prior to trial after having paid a certain amount of money—referred to as bail or bond.

In the years since Washington's arrest, reformers have succeeded in altering the way the bail system works in Saint Louis. Now an arrested person is guaranteed a bond hearing within forty-eight hours of his or her detention, and the bail amount is based on the person's financial means. But in 2018 a judge set Washington's bail at $150,000, citing the seriousness of the charges. To be freed until his day in court, the trucker would have to put up the entire amount. In cash. In other words, he wasn't getting out.

Washington had been locked up about two weeks when his case was finally assigned a lawyer. Public defender Ryan Hehner's first priority was to convince the judge to lower the bond amount. The facts of the case, he argued, showed that while the charges made it sound like Washington was a dangerous, violent criminal, even the police's version of events made it clear that the incident resulted from a mutual misunderstanding.

The judge agreed, reducing Washington's bond to $5,000, which the Bail Project agreed to pay. The national nonprofit organization helps finance the release of cash-strapped suspects and has bailed more than 1,300 people out of the Workhouse. Washington was so relieved when he got the news that he went back to his cell block and hurriedly packed up his things in silence.

For three months, he had thought of almost nothing else except how he'd get out. But even after his release, he remained pinned beneath the weight of his incarceration. Being separated from the free world for three months had cost him nearly everything.

The landlords of his apartment in Indianapolis, having assumed that he was dead, dragged his belongings to the curb. The 2004 Mercedes he'd bought just weeks before his arrest had been repossessed when Washington's loan payments stopped going through. Gone too was the semitruck he'd been a week away from purchasing. And with the criminal charges still pending, there was no chance he could get another job driving trucks.

Washington was released while Saint Louis was in the midst of an arctic chill, with temperatures dipping into the single digits and even lower overnight. His attorney worried that Washington would be ordered back to the Workhouse if he couldn't find housing or, worse, freeze to death. For three days, Washington wandered from homeless shelter to homeless shelter before finally finding an open basement cot for $200 a week. He cobbled together the rent by taking spare handyman and carpentry gigs. He spent his days lifting weights, looking for work, and passing time on the arcade-style Ms. Pac-Man machine set up against the back wall of the dreary basement. "Life is a lot like these games. Life has a lot of traps," he remarked one afternoon as he played. "You go through the wrong door and get bit by a ghost."

He'd found a bed, but rest remained elusive. Lingering injuries to his shoulder and neck made it hard to doze off. Nightmares in which officers opened fire at him or dragged him from his truck made it impossible to sleep soundly. Some nights he'd take an extra sip of liquor as he lay his head back on his thin pillow, praying he'd be able to drift into intoxicated slumber. Still, even on those nights, he'd jolt awake, trapped in the despondent space between drunk and hungover, his body covered in cold sweat.

A few weeks after his release, Washington received a call from his public defender. The Bail Project was cohosting a public forum regarding the year-old campaign to close the Workhouse. It would mean a lot to the organizers, Ryan Hehner explained to him, if he would come share his story.

Washington was eager to help however he could. At the March forum, he stood up and told his story to the few dozen attendees. Afterward, he mingled with members of the crowd, which is when he was approached by Kim Gardner, the recently elected city prosecutor.

Gardner, the first black person to ever hold the position, had been swept into office in 2016 along with a class of prosecutors who vowed to champion criminal justice reform. Gardner instructed her office to decline prosecution for a number of low-level drug offenses and had specifically pledged to decrease the use of incarceration as a penalty for relatively minor offenses. Unknowingly, Washington had placed himself in front of the person with the near-singular power to save him.

The two shook hands and spoke briefly; then she listened in from a distance as he explained the details of his case to another attendee. When Gardner got back to her office, she looked up Washington's case and read through the file. "We have a duty to pursue justice, not convictions," Gardner told me when I asked her about the case later. Ninety days in jail, she concluded, was more than enough punishment. "I made a decision that I think we should do something differently."

The event had been held on a Tuesday evening. On Friday afternoon, Washington's phone rang. It was his attorney. The charges had all been dropped. He no longer faced any jail time.

Who did you talk to? Hehner asked.

Well, said Washington, I spoke with that lady from the prosecutor's office.

That lady *was* the prosecutor! Hehner explained.

The charges were gone for good. Washington didn't respond. He'd fallen to his knees, crying on the floor.

27

IT WOULD BE NICE IF Shawn Washington's story had ended there. A ribbon-tied ending, a tale of triumph. But the cruel reality facing activists and reformers is that for each person they free, many more remain incarcerated. For each inequality they rid from the system, another emerges in its place. Even though he'd dodged the worst of what could have come from his brush with police and his time in the Workhouse, the incident had still upended Washington's life. The tears kept coming over the next few months, only they were no longer an outpouring of joy but rather an overflow of frustration.

Washington had assumed that the charges being dropped would be enough to secure another truck driving job. But company after company rejected him. The incident was showing up on his record, and even though he wielded an official letter from Gardner declaring the case dismissed, would-be employers remained unwilling to take the chance.

He found a gig working maintenance at an apartment building on the city's east side, but the neighborhood was so rough he knew he had to find something else. The building was constantly flooded with police and federal gun agents investigating cases, and he'd often pause in the middle of fixing tenants' overhead lights and leaking refrigerators to gauge the closeness of gunshots from outside. One night he exited the building after a particularly long shift to discover that his truck had been stolen from its parking spot.

Eager to escape the environment, Washington took a job in Chicago fixing heating and cooling units. But he discovered quickly that the operation was shady, with the workers being paid under the table—that is, when they were paid at all. Soon he was back in Saint Louis. Not long after that, his money ran out.

Washington refused to sleep under the overpasses and couldn't bring himself to stand on a corner with a cardboard sign. Instead, he made his way to an abandoned house with a FOR SALE sign on the door. After climbing in through a window, he found the place trashed, but at least there was a mold-covered mattress on the floor of one of the bedrooms. Washington didn't tell his ex-wife or parents that he was homeless, but, knowing he was low on cash, they'd order him a pizza every other day that he would pick up from the Little Caesars around the corner.

For three months, he spent his days at the nearby McDonald's, using the restaurant's outlets to charge his phone and its Wi-Fi to apply for jobs. When the workers weren't looking, he'd sneak splashes of soda from the machine. At night, he'd climb back through the window to see how much of the pizza from the night before had been devoured by the family of racoons that had taken up as his roommates.

Then, one morning in September, he was jolted awake by the buzz of a lawn mower outside. The homeowners had returned. Washington hid in the house, knowing his residency was likely over for good. When the coast was clear, he snuck out through the window and returned to McDonald's to figure out what to do now. An older man breathing through a portable oxygen tank, likely a resident from the senior home up the street, offered Washington his extra cookie. Perhaps, Washington desperately hoped, this was a sign.

Moments later, his phone rang. It was the hiring manager for an Alabama-based trucking company. Was he still interested in the job? "I'm going to be straight with you," Washington told the man, not willing to risk getting his hopes up. "There's something on my record. But the charges have been dropped."

That wasn't a problem, the hiring manager assured him. Hours later, Washington was at the public library, faxing over a copy of the letter Garner had written to confirm that his criminal record was clean. Just days after that, the company emailed him a Greyhound bus ticket to its training program in Nashville. He was a driver again.

28

I'M NOT SURE WHEN, EXACTLY, the tradition began. Most likely, it was during one of my many trips to Ferguson in 2014 and 2015. But in recent years, anytime I've been dispatched to cover a police shooting and the unrest that has sprung up in response, I've made it a ritual to begin my visit to the city at the scene of the shooting. Most times, I get a car directly there after landing at the airport. There's something about being among the protesters, who undoubtedly are still gathered at the scene, that steels me with the energy such an assignment will require. There's something about remembering that no matter where the news cycle has gone—the politicians' response, the policy debates, outrage at rioting and violence—this is a story, fundamentally, about someone whose life has been lost.

And so, after I landed in Minneapolis in June 2020, I made my way to the corner of Thirty-Eighth Street and Chicago Avenue, where, days before, Officer Derek Chauvin had kneeled on George Floyd's neck for nine and a half minutes. Then the forty-six-year-old victim stopped breathing.

For years, protesters in this city had taken to the streets to demand a wholesale reimagining of the criminal justice system. And Floyd's death, combined with that of Breonna Taylor, a black woman shot and killed by police in Louisville earlier in the year, would force a national and international reckoning of a scale previously unseen and, in fact, unimaginable.

In the weeks I spent in Minneapolis that summer, it was hard not to think back, with some sorrow, on the great pain and sacrifice required to bring this city to this point. It had been a half-decade fight, built atop years of prior activism that was happening all around the country. There had been massive protests in Minneapolis in 2014, for example, in the aftermath of Michael Brown's killing. And in the years to come, those same protesters would be thrust back into the streets time and again, after police killings of their fellow Minnesotans: I'd first come to Minneapolis in November 2015, after police shot and killed Jamar Clark, a twenty-four-year-old unarmed black man. Hundreds poured into the streets in what were then some of the largest protests the country had seen since Ferguson the year before.

But thinking back on the story of Jamar Clark's death and the resultant protests was a reminder not just of the gruesome toil of the movement, but also of the violent, white supremacist backlash that it would inspire.

On November 15 Jamar Clark had been at a birthday party when the fight broke out. Like most stories of an intoxicated altercation, the details remain a little murky and vary, depending on who you talk to. The birthday girl, and hostess, ended up in an argument with her husband. Clark's girlfriend, who was also at the party, intervened, grabbing the birthday girl. Before long, the two women were fighting. When Clark stepped in to pull his girlfriend away, he ended up on the receiving end of a punch from her.

Paramedics and police arrived and placed Clark's girlfriend in the back of an ambulance. When he approached the ambulance, police told him to stop. This is where the stories diverge.

According to a number of eyewitness accounts, officers jumped out of their cars, threw Clark to the ground, handcuffed him, and then shot him. The officers, in their statements, said that Clark was not handcuffed, that he refused to show them his hands, and that he resisted their attempts to take him into custody. It was only after Clark and Officer Mark Ringgenberg ended up scuffling on the ground, and Clark made a move for the policeman's gun, that his partner, Dustin Schwarze, opened fire.

Local prosecutors would ultimately decline to bring charges against the officers, while federal investigators concluded that Clark was likely not handcuffed but that the witness accounts were too inconsistent to determine precisely what had happened that night.

As authorities investigated, hundreds of people took to the streets, occupying the blocks outside of the local police precinct. They demanded that any and all video of the incident be released publicly, that there be an investigation into the police response to the protests, and that the officers involved be criminally charged. "It was the case of Jamar Clark that really brought a bunch of attention," Miski Noor, a leader with the local Black Lives Matter chapter, told me later. "It was the moment folks were, like, Minneapolis is a place to pay attention to."

Among those taking to the streets was Jamar Clark's cousin Cameron Clark. He'd seen the flashing police car lights that night and heard that someone had been killed, but it wasn't until the next morning that he learned the victim was his cousin. "I was devastated," Cameron told me. "He was a calm, cool, collected guy. If Jamar was going through the struggle, you would never know 'cause he's always smiling and telling jokes." Even more than five years later, Cameron told me, he still loses sleep over Jamar's death.

The demonstrations were the first time that Clark had joined a protest. He marched and he shouted. He was hit with tear gas and rubber bullets when officers attempted to clear the streets. The entire thing reminded him of the documentaries he'd been shown in school of Martin Luther King and police turning fire hoses on civil rights demonstrators of the 1960s. The only difference, it seemed, was that no K-9s had been set loose on them. He gave interviews calling for the officers to be arrested and charged. "But I know how the justice system is," he said to me. "Things did not go in our favor at all."

For a week, Clark and other protesters stayed camped outside of the police department's Fourth District Precinct. Things were tense. Protesters braced for another violent police response, as there were growing calls for clearing the streets—including online threats on white supremacist forums. If the police wouldn't get the agitators out of the streets, the posters wrote, they would do it themselves.

"We're blockin' this police station, and, at the same time, white supremacists were comin' to harm us," recalled Jason Cole, a key organizer in the protests. "But, at the same time, it was, like, we just felt we had to stay there, and we had to listen to the family. The family wanted us to be there."

Then, on the night of November 23, at around 10:40 p.m., four white men, most of them wearing masks, showed up. "They're around just taking pictures, just lurking around," Clark recalled. He'd been passing out food to fellow demonstrators at the time and watched as other organizers tried to speak to the men. The encampment, strictly self-governed, had rules, one of them being that strangers couldn't come wearing masks.

An argument broke out, and Clark ran over to try to cool the tension. They attempted to force the outsiders up the street, away from the protests. But as the men made their exit, one of them, twenty-three-year-old Allen Lawrence Scarsella, turned around, produced a gun, and opened fire. The protesters scattered. As he ran, Cameron was struck twice: once in the right leg and once in his left foot.

• • •

Police ultimately arrested four white men in connection with the attack. But it was Scarsella who faced the most serious charges. He had fired eight shots, wounding five protesters.

After the shooting, Scarsella called a friend and told him that he had just shot five people. Hours later, a call came in to local police from an officer at a different department who knew Scarsella personally. The suspect, he explained, had called him to confess to the crime and also to ask for advice.

Police found Scarsella at his home. When they searched his cell phone, the internal GPS confirmed that he had been outside the police precinct that night. And among his text messages were conversations with the other men present that night detailing their plans to disrupt the protests. In one text message, produced later by prosecutors, Scarsella bragged that he had a gun specifically designed to kill black people. They also found photos of him posing with a Confederate flag. In online comments on the anonymous forum 4chan, Scarsella disparaged the growing protests and discussed what he believed was a coming race war.

After reviewing surveillance video, police determined that Scarsella had previously crashed the protests to film the demonstrators and argue with them. He had filmed himself and a friend on the way to the protest, dressed in camouflage, declaring that they were going to "make the fire rise" and "do some reverse cultural enriching."

During the trial, prosecutors would provide trails of digital evidence to document that Scarsella was clearly racist.

"Someone needs to go down there and make all those dumb niggers afraid to leave the safety of their homes," he wrote in a March 12, 2015, text message referencing Black Lives Matter protesters. Just hours before the shooting, Scarsella sent a message to his girlfriend complaining that Sam's Club was "packed with smelly brown people walking too slow."

Scarsella was found guilty. "The fact that others were injured because of something I did weighs heavily on my heart every day," he told the judge prior to his sentencing. "The incident touched so many lives, and everybody who was involved is now worse off for it." Ultimately, he was given fifteen years in prison.

Two days after the shooting, the day before Thanksgiving, Jamar Clark's family gathered at the Shiloh Temple, an international Pentecostal congregation just blocks from where he had died, to hold a funeral. Even with the police accountability protests raging, even in light of the white supremacist attack on the protesters, this was still the story of a man who had been killed. Among the first words spoken at the service were Jamar's own.

"I haven't been feeling good, but not, like, sick; more, like, time is running out," the twenty-four-year-old wrote in his final Facebook status update, which was read aloud by a friend standing a few feet from Clark's casket. "Like, I don't have too much time, but I know I have some type of purpose on this earth." He was the youngest of ten kids, and the third of his parents' children to die. His obituary testified to his love for swimming and fishing, noted that he had been working for a local trucking company and car wash, and recalled that "as a child, Jamar was always full of energy and had a big smile."

For many of the families of those killed by police, the gale of scrutiny and attention—a burden that comes as they prepare to bury their loved one—is overwhelming.

At the memorial, one of Jamar's sisters fought back tears as she urged mourners not to take their loved ones for granted. Their dead relatives become hashtags, characters whose lives are publicly dissected both by those seeking to lionize the dead and those seeking to demonize them. Whether they wish it or not, each loved one's funeral service doubles as a public event that is equal parts grieving and politicking.

About a hundred people sat in purple velvet pews, some in dark suits but many more in T-shirts calling for "Justice for Jamar" or emblazoned with his likeness. As they spoke one at a time of the brother, cousin, or son they'd lost, the family members could not divorce their slain loved one from the symbol he had now become in death. They praised the ongoing protests, they called on local elected officials to demonstrate leadership, and they insisted that justice required that the officers be charged.

"Jamar, your life did and does have purpose," shouted Bishop Richard Howell. "Your death was not in vain!"

I ZIPPED UP MY JACKET tight against the crisp November breeze as I crossed the street to meet Dr. Jalane Schmidt on a corner just east of the Charlottesville courthouse. The first thing she wanted to show me was a seven-foot-tall horse trough.

According to the inscription on a plaque a few feet away, the city first installed four downtown water fountains like this one in the late 1800s, each with a lower bowl for smaller domesticated animals such as dogs to drink from and a higher bowl that pooled water for horses. This particular bowl, at Sixth Street and East Jefferson Street, is bold and black with complex engraving and was restored by the city in 2004.

"This feature here, that's seven foot tall? We have more material evidence of horses here than of the humans who were sold here," Schmidt told me as we glanced up at the fancy water fountain.

Charlottesville and the rest of Albemarle County—home to Thomas Jefferson's Monticello plantation—had been 52 percent black at the time of the Civil War, with fourteen thousand enslaved people and another six hundred free black people. And yet, in a city full of Confederate iconography, the only notation of the city's black population from that time was a small sidewalk marker. To walk around the city would leave you with the impression that it was a significant Confederate stronghold. You'd have no idea that it was, functionally, a black city. Revisionist history has long been one of white supremacy's favored weapons.

"Over half the population here, at the time of the Civil War, were enslaved," remarked Schmidt. Pointing to the water foundation memorial, she noted, "There are a hundred nineteen words on that plaque. And there's one little one for the slaves that's got, like, seven words on it." That is, when the little plaque commemorating the enslaved black people who were bought and sold in Charlottesville's city center hasn't been stolen or vandalized. But when it's there, the small marker embedded in the sidewalk just around the corner from the horse fountain contains eleven words: "Slave auction block: On this site slaves were bought and sold."

Schmidt, a local activist and professor at the University of Virginia, is among a group of local historians who have taken it upon themselves to recontextualize Charlottesville's public iconography and highlight the contradictions of its city's history. By the time we met up in late 2020, Schmidt had been giving this tour for more than two years.

We walked up the street to what had once been the Eagle Tavern, one of the city's first hotels. The two-story wooden building was now used primarily for dinners, concerts, and public dances. It was here, in 1829, that thirty-three enslaved people who had once been owned by Jefferson were sold by his grandson, in the largest known slave auction ever held in Charlottesville. "There's nothing here that marks that," Schmidt observed as we stood in the spot where these families were sold. A few hundred feet away stood a sign noting that we were just three miles from Monticello. "Evidence of the kind of priority that the city has about public history," Schmidt commented. When she and others held a vigil at the site a few years ago, they had the names of each of the thirty-three enslaved people read off by Myra Anderson, a local poet who can trace her lineage back to the Hern family—six of the enslaved who were sold here.

We'd spend the next two hours like this, walking up and down the streets of Charlottesville, taking note of what history this city had chosen to remember and what parts of its past had been more convenient to forget. As the journalist and poet Clint Smith notes in *How the Word Is Passed: A Reckoning with the History of Slavery Across America*, "The echo of enslavement is everywhere." In Charlottesville, those echoes are impossible to quiet.

Across the street from the former auction block stands a new memorial commemorating the 1898 lynching of a black man named John Henry James, an ice cream vendor who was falsely accused of assaulting a white woman and murdered by a mob of 150 white men. Some of the killers took home pieces of the tree where he had hung—as well as parts of James's body—as souvenirs. No one was ever charged criminally for his murder.

It was around this time, Schmidt explained, that Charlottesville began changing. In the years following emancipation, the local black population had eagerly begun attending schools and launching businesses. But amid a wave of racial terror like James's lynching, black residents soon began moving away, part of what we now know as the Great Migration, in which black families that had formerly been enslaved in the South moved to the North, Midwest, and West. By 1890, the city was no longer majority black. And in 1902 the state legislature approved a new constitution implementing a poll tax that had to be paid six months before Election Day and ultimately disenfranchised about 90 percent of the state's black voters.

It was during this era of whitelash—the era of white supremacist Redemption that followed the post–Civil War Reconstruction—that Charlottesville became home to its expansive slate of Confederate iconography. Legacies, after all, are constructed from not just those things we choose to remember and those things we endeavor to conceal, but also from the spots where in the position of history we instead place fiction. Our history is simply a story that we tell ourselves. So often the tale that we tell is a lie.

Just up the street, there once stood the statue known as "Johnny Reb": a monument depicting a Confederate soldier standing at the ready with rifle in hand, constructed in 1909. On the day of its dedication, a crowd gathered to sing "Dixie," the anthem of the Confederacy, and wave the Stars and Bars. As the dedication speech given by a Confederate veteran made clear, this was not a monument constructed to honor the fallen troops but rather the cause of white supremacy and its return under Jim Crow. Among those involved in its commissioning was the prosecutor who had declined to bring any criminal charges in John Henry James's lynching.

Around the corner, on the opposite side of the courthouse from the James memorial, stood a statue to Confederate general Stonewall Jackson, installed outside the courthouse in 1921, a time when Southern whites were forcefully asserting racial segregation and a white supremacist hierarchy via Jim Crow. The Jackson statue, Schmidt explained to me, sent a message to the black people of Charlottesville as they approached the courthouse. It was a reminder, carved in stone for everyone to see, that they were second-class citizens. On the day we spoke, Schmidt told me, seventy-five Confederate monuments still sat in front of courthouses in the state of Virginia.

The Jackson statue was one of several commissioned by Paul Goodloe McIntire, a philanthropist whose father had been the city's mayor during the Civil War. Another, of General Robert E. Lee, stood just a few blocks up the street.

The irony of all of it, Schmidt noted, was that Charlottesville wasn't a major theater of war. The men memorialized so prominently here—Generals Jackson and Lee—never once visited the city. The fact is that when it fell to Union forces, the majority of those living in Charlottesville would have been elated.

"The outright majority of the population here was enslaved. I never get tired of saying that," Schmidt told me as we headed toward the courthouse. "There were all of these people coming here—you know, reporters, coming here after the summer of hate—saying, 'Well, why Charlottesville?' There is a whole deep history here."

30

TO UNDERSTAND THE SUMMER OF hate, we have to first rewind more than a year to March 2016, when fifteen-year-old Zy Bryant received a ninth-grade essay assignment.

The instructions were to write about something that she could change. For many students, the papers ended up being about topics such as recycling. But Bryant decided she wanted hers to be different. She kept thinking about Charlottesville and its public spaces. She hated that some parts of the city weren't welcoming to everyone. She thought specifically about Lee Park—which she had visited on field trips but which certainly didn't feel like the kind of place where she was welcome.

In 1917 McIntire had bought the land now known as Lee Park, cleared it, and commissioned the statue of Lee riding atop his horse. The twenty-six-foot-tall monument was unveiled seven years later, in May 1924—and would remain in this place of prominence, at the center of the city, for nearly a century.

Bryant had long been aware of race, taking note that she was one of the only black students in her private school elementary classes. She'd lived in Charlottesville her entire life, and her family for generations before that. But could they ever feel truly at home in a city that so prominently honored a man who had enslaved people and fought to defend the evil institution?

Bryant turned in her paper and received a good grade. But she couldn't stop wondering if there was a way she could turn the demand she'd made in her essay into more tangible, impactful action. And so she crafted an online petition calling for the local city council to rename the park and to take down the statue. Later, she sent it in to the local paper as a letter to the editor. "There is more to Charlottesville than just the memories of Confederate fighters. There is more to this city that makes it great," she wrote. "Let's not forget that Robert E. Lee fought for perpetual bondage of slaves and the bigotry of the South that kept most black citizens as slaves and servants for the entirety of their lives. As a result, legislatures of the South chose to ignore and turn a blind eye to the injustices of African Americans from Jim Crow and antiblack terrorism to integrated education. These are all some things that this statue stands for."

Within an hour, a classmate of Bryant's, a girl she had known since middle school, had taken to Facebook to decry the petition. "There is nothing wrong with the statue," the girl wrote. "This is what's wrong with Black Lives Matter."

Bryant was stunned. The post didn't feel like the politics of someone her age, all of whom she had assumed shared her progressive values. "I hadn't really understood the way politics were passed down through families," she would tell me later. Charlottesville was a quiet, liberal college town. One of the Democratic strongholds of the state. But Virginia is a southern state, after all. And it didn't take long for the opposition to grow. Another classmate posted similar comments. Then another. Commenters were calling her a carpetbagger and a "libtard." Bryant was young, but to these online avatars, she was everything wrong with progressives and the Left.

However, the momentum that she'd gotten rolling continued to pick up speed. In May 2016 city councilman Wes Bellamy cited Bryant's petition and the signatures she had gathered as the catalyst for the creation of a Blue Ribbon Commission on Race, Memorials, and Public Spaces, to determine whether the statues honoring Lee and Jackson should remain in place. Six months later, the nine-member commission voted 6 to 3 to keep the statues in place, although it did recommend renaming Lee Park. But the city council had other ideas, voting 3 to 2 in favor of removing the monuments.

By then, the opposition had grown beyond Facebook comments, and several groups, including the Sons of Confederate Veterans, immediately sued the city to prevent the statues from being taken down. While the case worked its way through the legal system, the statues were to remain standing. But the controversy continued to burn as 2016 gave way to 2017.

Charlottesville is a deep blue dot in the middle of what is otherwise a deeply conservative section of Virginia. More than 80 percent of the vote here went for Hillary Clinton in 2016, and President Trump's victory provoked an emotional, outraged response. When the Women's March was held in Washington, DC, the day following the inauguration, Charlottesville sent about fifty busloads of protesters to the capital. And when Trump instituted the Muslim ban a short time later, residents grew even more agitated.

"This is not funny," declared Charlottesville mayor Mike Signer during a public rally. "These folks couldn't run a two-car parade much less policies affecting the rights and lives of millions of people, and that is why I am here today to declare that Charlottesville, the historical home of Thomas Jefferson, is a capital of the resistance."

But the Trump election had been a radicalizing event not just for Charlottesville's liberals but also for the white supremacist movement, and the simmering fight over the city's Confederate monuments had made the city their rallying point. Corey Stewart, who had helped run Trump's campaign in Virginia, made the issue central to his bid for the Republican nomination for governor—propelling him from a longshot to within a couple thousand votes of victory. Before long, he and other white supremacist leaders became regular features in town. "There was a direct connection between the hate that Trump was kicking up, and what happened on our streets right here," Jalane Schmidt told me.

For months, the city had hosted forums and meetings about the future of the statues. Zy Bryant worked hard to remain a typical teen—doing homework and going to softball practice—in between attending the council meetings every other week. "These things are very bizarre," she recalls. "There were white people coming to these meetings dressed up in full Civil War–era costumes." To take down the statues, these people argued, was to erase history. The statues, they said, were gorgeous pieces of equestrian art. Sitting near the back of many of the meetings was a local activist named Jason Kessler.

Zy Bryant was sitting in tenth-grade chemistry class in May 2017 when her phone began lighting up with the news. White supremacist groups were planning a demonstration in Charlottesville.

The event had been called by Richard Spencer—then the most recognizable racist in the country after having gained fame for leading his followers in Nazi salutes after Trump's victory—and Kessler, who had been among the most vocal local opponents of the plan to take down the statues. Dozens of demonstrators met at Lee Park, lit torches, and marched through the city. Among the chants heard were "Blood and soil!"—a Nazi slogan—and variations of "You will not replace us!" and "Jews will not replace us!"

"I think one thing that I have in common with all of you here today is that I don't give a goddamn about being called a racist," Kessler reportedly told the crowd that gathered, in which the assembled racists far outnumbered counterprotesters.

"They're talking in both coded and noncoded language," explained Ibby Han, a key activist who helped organize counterprotests throughout that spring and summer. While many of the speeches were specifically about the Confederate statues, others veered into other white supremacist talking points: the breakdown of the family structure, the destructive nature of unchecked immigration, the supremacy of the white race. "Their rallying cry was about the statues, but underneath that there was so much more," Han said. "Preserving their Aryan European culture. 'You will not replace us' sort of sentiment."

The local activists vowed to not be outnumbered again. On July 8, when a group of Klansmen held a demonstration and rally in Lee Park, the counterprotesters showed up in force.

"There's probably thirty to forty people in the KKK entourage . . . being escorted by the cops," Han recalled. "We had probably a thousand people there. It was a noise demonstration—people brought instruments, trombones, drums. No one could hear anything that the Klan members were saying. Even the people next to them couldn't hear what they were saying. We were able to totally drown them out."

The Klansmen were escorted away from the scene by police, who would later deploy tear gas against the counterdemonstrators, infuriating them. "That was the day where everyone was, like, it's super clear the cops are only here to protect white supremacists and property; they aren't ever going to protect us from the violence that the white supremacists are going to enact," Han told me. But all in all, the evening was relatively uneventful—at least compared with the chaos yet to come.

For months, Kessler had fashioned himself the enemy of Bryant, Bellamy, and the cadre of activists fighting to remove Charlottesville's Confederate monuments. Now, emboldened by the support he felt at the torch rally, he put in for a permit for another, even larger assembly called Unite the Right, and planned for August 2017. He promoted it as a free speech rally. But those who had been following the events in Charlottesville and taking note of the increasingly emboldened posture of the white supremacist movement in the months since Trump had assumed office knew that violence was likely.

"People think that they're largely ignorant, that they don't know what they're doing, these are people who are just white lower-class people who think 'The South will rise again.' No, these are well-established white people," Bryant told me. "These are people who are judges, professors, elected officials from different towns, city council people. These are people who are well established; people who are in positions to make decisions. These are people who are in positions to actually influence the next generation."

The Unite the Right rally did not really have to happen. Local activists begged the mayor and the city council to pull the permit. It was clear, they argued, that this was no free speech rally but rather was almost certainly going to end in mob violence. Some of the activists presented to city officials printouts of the threats of violence they'd found online from those planning to attend the event. White supremacists from across the country had answered the call and were openly declaring that they were planning to be in Charlottesville. Anti-racist demonstrators, horrified by the video clips from the May torch rally, were also driving to the site of the rally to counter it. The city tried to move the rally to a larger location. But Kessler, with the help of the ACLU, forced it back to its original location.

"We started to get outside attention," Bryant recalled. "Charlottesville became the topic of conversation: 'These liberals are trying to rewrite history.'"

The teenager thought it was all pretty ridiculous. She was getting death threats and being named on white supremacist message boards. Some of the other activists she had met in the year since she'd written her essay were even more under siege, having their personal information circulated online, resulting in waves of threatening messages.

"Do these people not have anything else to do?" Bryant thought. "I'm fifteen and sixteen, I'm actually trying to be in high school, and I'm getting death threats." How far, she wondered, were these people willing to go?

The Friday night before Unite the Right, the white supremacists gathered secretly on the University of Virginia campus for a torch rally and march. The assembly was unannounced, but it wasn't long before the plans had been leaked to the local anti-racist groups. About thirty counterprotesters headed to the Thomas Jefferson statue that sits in the university rotunda, which was where the march was set to end, while Han and a handful of others went to UVA to see how many white supremacists had assembled.

Standing on a patio that overlooked the campus field where the white supremacists had gathered, Han saw Kessler and what looked like about fifty supporters. But when she got a better view, there were at least three hundred of them. Maybe more. They were all dressed in white polo shirts and khaki pants and carrying tiki torches. "Oh, shit, how do we possibly . . . what do you do with that? How do you shut that down?" Han recalled thinking. "I was just scared and panicked and thinking of my friends who were all at the statue who had no idea what was coming for them." She raced back to the Jefferson statue to tell the others how many white supremacists were on their way, and the decision was made that they would all link arms and hold the space around the statue.

The ensuing confrontation was predictably chaotic. The white supremacists arranged in formation, marching two by two to the Thomas Jefferson statue as they shouted their bigoted chants. When they encountered the student protesters, the white supremacists circled them, yelling, "White lives matter!" A brawl broke out between white supremacists and counterprotesters. Some of the white supremacists had brought along pepper spray. Eventually the police, who had largely stayed off to the side, declared an unlawful assembly and began using pepper spray to disperse everyone, at least for the rest of the night.

31

ON THE MORNING OF AUGUST 12, 2017, Zy Bryant woke early to attend a five o'clock interfaith sunrise service the local activists had planned. She watched and listened as activists she had spent more than a year working with sorted into pairs. Today would be dangerous, they were all told. Were they willing to die for this cause? The emotion and seriousness hung heavy in the air.

Because she had been specifically named in some of the online threats, Bryant was not out on the streets that day. Instead, she holed up in a safe location, watching events unfold on multiple televisions, with CNN on one screen and MSNBC on another.

Hundreds of people, on both sides, showed up that day, clashing up and down the streets of Charlottesville's scenic downtown. White supremacists had brought clubs, poles, guns, sticks, and shields, while some counterdemonstrators wore protective riot gear. Others carried little more than cardboard signs.

"People didn't take the activists seriously when we said we needed to deplatform them," Han recalled. "But at this point, not too long into the Trump administration, people were still, like, 'If we just ignore them, they'll go away. All we need to do is not give them any air and ignore them.'" The city had ignored them, ill-advisedly granting the white supremacists a protest permit. Now there were hundreds of them parading through the streets. "That is a tactic that works sometimes," reflected Han, "but this was not one of those times, because they had gained so much momentum. . . . Every town has their local racist who makes their annoying comments at city council, but this was different." Kessler, she said, "was able to bring all of these scary people together."

The twenty-two-year-old Han had been placed in charge of what the activists were calling an off-site medical facility set up in a church bordering Lee Park. The Unite the Right rally was supposed to begin at noon, but the white supremacist protesters had gathered beginning as early as eight thirty that morning. By nine thirty, Han's medical team was seeing a steady stream of injured counterprotesters. Lacerations. Bruises. Eyes burning from pepper spray. The white supremacists had shown up ready to fight. Some had their knuckles taped. Others carried wooden poles, bats, and helmets. Still others, guns and knives.

Throughout the morning, Han would go out with another medical volunteer, driving loops through the city and picking up injured counterdemonstrators. Virginia governor Terry McAuliffe declared a state of emergency, and the Virginia State Police— overwhelmed and seemingly unprepared for the violent chaos— declared an unlawful assembly at Lee Park, driving both the white supremacists and the counterprotesters down a series of side streets. The violence continued on sidewalks, in parking garages, and at intersections where the groups ran into each other.

As morning turned to afternoon, there was a celebratory atmosphere among many of the counterprotesters who had shown up. The rally had been canceled before it had a chance to get started. And now, counterprotesters marched through the streets, chanting and singing. Among them was a thirty-two-year-old woman named Heather Heyer. She'd spent the day away from most of the violence, joining a group that was singing and chanting several blocks away from the violence surrounding Lee Park. But as she marched to the downtown shopping area to continue the celebration, the day's violence would soon find her.

• • •

Heather Heyer had planned to skip the counterdemonstrations on the day of the Unite the Right rally. But the night before, as she and her friend Justin Scott, an African American, watched a livestream of the torch-wielding white supremacists, she felt moved to action. She felt she needed to be there. "If you're not outraged," Heyer wrote on Facebook, "you're not paying attention."

And so now, with the white supremacists largely disrupted and dispersed, Heyer and the other anti-racist activists worked their way up Fourth Street. Unbeknownst to them, a twenty-year-old white supremacist named James Alex Fields was sitting in his Dodge Challenger just up the hill from them—waiting for the right moment.

Fields had driven to Unite the Right from his home in Ohio. He had a history of mental illness and violence. It was unclear that he was a member of any of the groups involved in the rally's organization, but he'd long been obsessed with the white supremacist movement. Former classmates and teachers would recall later that Fields idolized Hitler. In 2016, one former teacher remembered, Fields had supported Donald Trump because of his cruel policies toward immigrants and Muslims.

As the counterprotesters celebrated, Fields accelerated into the crowd—police would later estimate making impact at a speed faster than twenty miles per hour—sending people flying into the air. He then put the vehicle in reverse, striking more pedestrians as he fled. At least thirty-five people were injured and one counterprotester, Heather Heyer, was killed.

Heather Heyer's death at the Unite the Right Rally made her a martyr of the anti-racist movement. By seven o'clock the next morning, reporters were knocking on the trailer door of her mother.

Susan Bro talked mostly about Heather, answering reporters' questions and hoping her daughter would be remembered for the life she'd lived. "When you lose a loved one, and someone says, 'Talk about your loved one,' you say, 'Sure, I'll talk about them.' You're happy to have someone listen as you grieve."

Her daughter had been wild and feisty and opinionated, known for talking with her hands waving in excitement. She was a Gemini: hard-nosed and badass. She had been outspoken, in recent years, about issues of racial justice. She'd debated with her mother about white privilege. Bro had a hard time grappling with the concept. She was white and had spent much of her adulthood living paycheck to paycheck on an elementary school teacher's salary.

Mother and daughter had both grown worried as they watched the rise of Donald Trump. Of particular alarm to Bro was the KKK rally in July. Back when she was in college, Bro and two friends had gotten lost along a back road and came upon a burning house. The house, the police and firefighters told them, belonged to a biracial couple, and had been set on fire by the local Klan. They were told to move along and forget what they had seen.

About an hour after Heyer was killed, President Trump read a prepared statement from his golf club in New Jersey. "We condemn in the strongest possible terms this egregious display of hatred, bigotry, and violence," he began. Then he ad-libbed "on many sides, on many sides." It was typical Trump, if confounding, even to many Republicans. There were not "many sides" to be condemned in Charlottesville. Just one side. The white supremacists.

Three days later, speaking at Trump Tower in New York, the president managed to make things worse, defending some of the white supremacists and seemingly taking up their cause.

"I think there is blame on both sides," he said, repeating himself. "You had a group on one side that was bad. You had a group on the other side that was also very violent. Nobody wants to say that. I'll say it right now. I've condemned neo-Nazis. I've condemned many different groups," he said. "Not all of those people were neo-Nazis, believe me. Not all of those people were white supremacists, by any stretch. Many of those people were there to protest the taking down of the statue of Robert E. Lee. So this week, it is Robert E. Lee. I noticed that Stonewall Jackson is coming down. I wonder, is it George Washington next week? And is it Thomas Jefferson the week after? You know, you really do have to ask yourself, where does it stop?"

Heather's funeral, Bro imagined, would be her last opportunity to say anything to a truly national audience. She had been working with Bell's Funeral Home, one of Charlottesville's oldest black-owned businesses. Heather would have wanted a service. The family didn't do churches, so Bro asked if they could think of a small venue. No, the staff at the funeral home responded, this event was going to be big.

Bro was specific about what she wanted. Local and state politicians could be there, but they would not speak. She wanted the media footprint to be small. Unobtrusive. When she arrived that morning, Bro was approached by a police officer. There was a bottleneck at the door, with a throng of people all claiming to be family and hoping to get in.

When she glanced at the crowd, Bro saw Heather's friends from her years waitressing, family friends, and local activists. Yeah, they're all family, she told the officer, who waved them all into the service. In total, more than a thousand people attended in person, and the service was carried live across most of the major cable news networks.

The service opened with words from Susan's best friend, Cathy Brinkley, who honored "a young woman who lost her life defending the rights of people." Next came Heather's grandfather, who recalled rocking her to sleep as a girl and making up silly songs to sing to her. "At an early age, she could call out something that didn't seem right to her," he recalled. "She wanted fairness, she wanted justice, she wanted everybody to get equal respect."

Through tears, her father told a story of a nine-year-old Heather arguing for two hours with her mother about not wanting to put on a sweater. "All I remember is Heather's passion," he said. "She wanted to put down hate."

About an hour into the funeral, it was time for Bro to make her way to the stage. She still hadn't had a chance to plan what she was going to say and took the podium without any speech or eulogy written down.

"I'm a speak-from-the-heart kind of person," she would tell me later. "Being a teacher, the thought going through my mind was, What are the lessons to learn here? What can we take away from this that's meaningful to the family, but also to the rest of the public?"

Bro recalled how her daughter loved to talk and debate. Politics, current events, the latest goings-on at work. Whatever it was, it always seemed Heather had a lot to say. And her mother heard more of it than anyone. "My child's famous Facebook post was 'If you're not outraged, you're not paying attention,'" Bro said. "She paid attention. She made a lot of us pay attention."

This entire service could have been small and private, Bro told the audience. But that wouldn't have been Heather. Her way was big and loud. "They tried to kill my child to shut her up. Well, guess what? You just magnified her," Bro declared, prompting raucous applause. Most importantly, she reminded those in attendance, was how normal Heather's actions had been. Any of them could have been in the streets, counterprotesting white supremacists on that day. And any of them could have, in turn, been the person killed.

"This is just the beginning of Heather's legacy. This is not the end of Heather's legacy. You need to find in your heart that small spark of accountability. What injustice do I see, and want to turn away [from seeing]—'I don't really want to get involved in that'—I don't care. You point that finger at yourself like Heather would have done. You find a way to make a difference in the world."

In the days after Heyer's death, a GoFundMe account was opened online to raise funds for her family. And after the telecast of her funeral, the amount raised skyrocketed to about $250,000.

Bro was shocked by how much money had come in, some of it in $4 and $5 donations sent directly to her trailer. She closed the account, paid off the remaining medical bills and funeral costs, and used what remained to start a foundation in Heather's name. Bro left her job, still overwhelmed by the press attention, to work for the foundation full-time.

It was a familiar path. Touched by tragedy, Bro had been thrust into a life of activism. "People started calling me an expert, and I don't know what the heck I'm doing," she recalled.

The U.S. Commission on Civil Rights invited her to attend an event, which led to an invitation to speak at the first gathering of the new Democratic House majority following the 2018 midterm elections. Next, she was invited to a panel about a proposal for new federal hate crime legislation. A group of families whose loved ones had been victims of hate crimes had come together to press for more accurate federal reporting. The FBI's statistics showed that hate crimes, in the first year of the Trump presidency, were on the rise for the third consecutive year. But the numbers, self-reported to the feds by local police departments, were woefully incomplete. Despite being perhaps the most high-profile murder victim in the country, Heyer had not been included in the official 2017 tally.

"To offer an accurate diagnosis, a doctor must have a full understanding of the symptoms. To adequately address the crisis of hate crimes, we need an accurate picture of how many hate crimes occur," Bro wrote in the statement she submitted to the U.S. House Committee on Oversight and Reform Subcommittee on Civil

Rights and Civil Liberties on May 15, 2019. "Accurate reporting of hate crime data will allow us to better combat this scourge of hate."

The proposed legislation aimed to improve hate crime reporting but also provided incentives for local municipalities and their police departments to participate. Part of the problem, civil rights groups have long believed, is that there are too many junctures throughout the process in which both the police and the victims themselves had reason to opt out. For cities and their police, there was plenty of reason to underreport such crimes: to begin with, gaining a reputation for tons of reported hate crimes wouldn't exactly be a boon for the local economy, property values, tourism, and so on. And though the federal government has requested such reporting for years, it was, in essence, an unfunded mandate. Many police departments simply did not devote the resources and attention required to ensure that their hate crime tallies were accurate. That tangible lack of effort only further incentivizes victims not to come forward. Hate crime victims are often among the most vulnerable a police department will ever encounter—targeted for their identity, victimized in intensely personal and degrading ways. Often it can feel easier to keep quiet. Especially if it feels like there is little that the police are going to do to help you—if they're not even going to record you among the official crime tally.

"Unfortunately, as politicians love to do it, it got tacked on with a whole wad," Bro noted. "They took the whole gumball and stuck it on the stimulus bill." For the time being, any momentum was stalled.

It would take two more years, and a new presidential administration and a Democratic Senate, but in May 2021 President Joe Biden signed new hate crime legislation into law—including provisions championed by Bro to improve hate crime reporting.

As she transitioned from grieving mother to activist, Susan Bro was also taking a more personal journey, an effort to more fully understand the historic forces that had swept up Charlottesville and cost her daughter her life. Heather had been the one paying attention. But now, Bro felt, it was her responsibility to listen and learn.

She'd quickly grown uncomfortable with so much of the way her daughter's death had been framed. She didn't know the term then, but she was sensing a "white savior complex": that her white daughter, in death, was becoming the face of a movement that had included thousands of anti-racist protesters, many of whom were black and brown.

In 2019 she discovered an organization called RISE, which had been founded by Sharon Fitz and Chanda McGuffin, two black women from Waynesboro, Virginia. Bro joined their forty-woman book club. The conversations were difficult and challenging.

"I was one of those people who thought that after Obama was elected that we were in a post-racial society. But if I'd started to think about it, I knew blacks and whites were not on equal footing," Bro told me. "When any of us is marginalized, we all are."

EPILOGUE

IN EARLY DECEMBER 2020 I boarded a train east from New York City and rode until it deposited me at a snowy train station in Patchogue. As I walked down the platform, I saw Joselo Lucero pull up. I hopped in his passenger seat and made small talk as he drove us out to a marina at the edge of town that sticks out into the Atlantic Ocean.

It had been nearly two years since the first time we had spoken. Much had changed, even as much had stayed depressingly the same.

"We thought we were part of the change in this country, it was something we celebrated," Joselo told me, looking out over the water and recalling his brother's murder, just days after Obama's election. And then came Trump.

Joselo told me that he has plenty of friends who supported Trump, and he was used to people on Long Island making excuses for his rhetoric. Trump is a New Yorker, after all. But Joselo never bought it. "When you are in power, no matter who you are, but when you've got that type of power, using rhetoric against immigrants, that's just putting fuel on the top of the fire," he said as we sat listening to the waves hit the dock.

He speaks carefully, deliberately. He said he had mixed feelings throughout the Trump years. Trump, he said, represented the fears of the average American. And that, in some ways, it was better to have those animosities out in the open. "Obama was able to encourage or create a little bit of empathy for immigrants in general," Joselo said. "The water was settled down a little bit. When Trump won, it was chaotic. Most people now don't think twice to say whatever comes to their mind. They don't have any fear of consequences."

Those chaotic four years—from the slander of immigrants and Muslims, to "very fine people on both sides" after Charlottesville—had been topped, in the weeks before my visit with Joselo, by Trump's "big lie": the insistence that he had not, in fact, lost the election and that it had been stolen from him. Neither of us knew then what was soon to come: the January 6 riot and insurrection, in which attendees of Trump's "Stop the Steal" rally would storm the U.S. Capitol building in an attempt to stop the certification of the electoral college tally.

A dozen years after his brother's death, Joselo told me he was disappointed by how few lessons seemed to have been learned. Sure, the intervening years had seen the rise of Black Lives Matter and more open conversations about discrimination and racism. But many of the same bigotries present for more than a century of right-wing populist politics, and that had poisoned the bloodstream of our politics in the years prior to Obama's election, were again on the rise in the post-Trump years: culture wars over how American history and anti-racism are taught; moral panics about gender and sexuality; a fresh round of demagoguery about immigrants, Muslims, and migrants; and a troubling wave of antisemitism in mainstream public discourse. With the 2024 presidential election fast approaching, it seems almost unquestionable that the race will come accompanied by the coarse, thoughtless rhetoric that plays into the ongoing American Whitelash and ultimately sets off more acts of white racial terror.

After about an hour, Joselo drove me back to the train station so I could grab a ride back into the city. As we pulled up, he took a quick detour to show me where a small plaque had at one point been laid at the spot where his brother had been killed. About a month earlier, on the anniversary of his brother's death, Joselo had gone there to place flowers, only to discover that the plaque had been stolen—his brother's memorial defaced.

One month later—and one week after the insurrection—I loaded the video feed to watch a sentencing hearing in Maryland, the final chapter in a story that had been playing out for the entirety of the Trump years. One of the first acts of racial violence that had caught my attention when I first began pondering the idea of American Whitelash was the 2017 murder of Richard Collins III.

His father, Rick Collins, told me that he had been up unusually early on the morning of Saturday, May 20, 2017—around seven o'clock. And so he decided to go out and check on his lawn sprinklers. It was a mundane weekend task. And the last moments he'd have that were unmarred by grief. Moments after returning inside, Collins heard the doorbell ring. Immediately, he thought of his son, Richard.

Just two days earlier, his son, Richard Collins III, had been commissioned into the army as a second lieutenant, and his family and friends had all gathered for a celebratory lunch. And the night before, Richard had headed out to the bars near the University of Maryland campus. He and a friend had set out around eleven at night to check out MilkBoy, a new bar downtown, before eventually making their way to Terrapin's Turf. After grabbing a slice of pizza, the two headed toward the nearby bus stop around three o'clock to head home.

Richard had told his father not to expect him back until sometime the following morning. And so Rick Collins imagined the possible scenarios as he walked to answer his front door: His son had probably forgotten his keys. Or maybe the code to the garage door wasn't working.

As Rick opened the door, his heart sank to his waist. On his stoop stood two Maryland State troopers. They looked no older than Richard. "I almost couldn't open my mouth," Rick would tell me later. "I knew right then that it was the worst."

The emotions began before he even had heard the news. Disbelief. Sadness. Horror. He wanted to appeal on his son's behalf. He wanted to find a way to make things right. But he knew, as he let the troopers in, that there was no changing what they had come here to tell him.

The troopers insisted Rick get his wife.

Rick and Dawn had first met decades before, as students at East Carolina University, set up by a mutual classmate. Married in 1985, they spent much of their early years apart. Rick was in the navy, gone six months at a time, during which their relationship was reduced to longing letters, care packages, and the occasional phone call when his ship reached port. It would be more than eight years before their firstborn son, Richard, came along in 1993.

Richard was inquisitive and precocious. Like most young boys in the 1990s, it was hard to separate him from his Game Boy. He was the type of kid who would respond to his mother's chidings by reminding her that the Bible instructs parents not to provoke their children to wrath. He had a philosophical streak and enjoyed the art of the argument. His mother might ask, "Richard, are you lying to me?" "Well, Mom," the boy would respond, "the Bible says that all men sin."

The Collinses were determined to invest the resources they had into Richard and his younger sister. That meant private schools and viola lessons. "All of the stuff that he hated," Rick recalled. "He played it only because he was made to." Eventually the viola gave way to lacrosse and soccer. And not long after that, he found another focus: following in the footsteps of his father and grandfather and entering the military. First, he joined the Coast Guard's high school program. But then Richard decided to go the ROTC route. He hoped to become an army officer one day. And so, Richard headed to Maryland's Bowie State University and enrolled in its Army ROTC program. "I saw him go to Bowie as a boy," Dawn remembered. "And the day of his commissioning, I saw a man."

After graduation, Richard was supposed to head off to Korea. He had big ambitions. Big plans. His eyes were set on becoming an army general. During one of the last conversations he had with his parents, he boasted, "Mom, you know one day I'm going to outrank Dad." To which his father replied, "Well, that might happen one day, but not today."

Now Rick and Dawn stood at the front door, braced to hear the news, even if they already knew in their guts what was coming. Their son had gone out the night before and never come home. What else could the officers at their door be here to relay? The troopers offered few details. Just that their son had died around three o'clock that morning.

It was only later that they would find out their son had been stabbed to death by Sean Urbanski, a white, twenty-two-year-old senior at the University of Maryland, in what was seemingly a random attack.

"I will tell you now that this case is an unspeakable tragedy for all concerned," defense attorney William C. Brennan told the twelve jurors who'd gathered December 11, 2019, to adjudicate the murder trial of Sean Urbanski. More than two and a half years had passed between Richard Collins's murder and the day that his parents were finally able to face their son's killer in court and hear from Urbanski's defense.

"It is an unspeakable tragedy for the Collins family, who have lost a son. It is a devastating tragedy for the Urbanski family, who will lose a son," Brennan said. "And it is also a tragedy, a demoralizing tragedy for the community, because the state has attempted to make this case something that it is not. The state has used race to divide this community."

Like the trial of Jeffrey Conroy in Patchogue a decade before, the proceedings were not meant as a litigation of the crime. By all accounts, Urbanski was drunk and angry that night. When police drew his blood the following morning, eight hours after the murder, his blood alcohol level was still .10—nearly twice the legal limit. (A legal expert for the defense would testify later that, at the time of the killing, it was likely three times the limit.) Everyone knew, everyone agreed, that Sean Urbanski had killed Richard Collins—the stabbing had been caught on a nearby surveillance camera. Collins's friends told the responding officers that the attacker had been a large white man wearing a green shirt and khaki shorts. When police found Urbanski a few minutes later, he was in a green shirt and khakis, with the bloody knife still clipped to his front pants pocket.

No, this case was not about whether Urbanski did it. The debate, to play out over three days of trial, was over *why*.

Even before all of the details had trickled out, Rick Collins *knew* what had happened to his son. It was a hate crime. A killing that occurred because of his son's skin color. It was the same thing, he was convinced, that had happened sixty-two years earlier to his own father.

In May 1954 Richard Collins Sr., twenty-three, had just gotten back from a tour of duty in Korea. He was recently married, and his son would arrive just a few months later. By the time Rick arrived, Richard Collins Sr. was dead.

His killer, a white man named J. C. Moore, told police that he had seen Collins looking into the window of one of his neighbors' houses in Tarboro, North Carolina, on May 14, 1954. According to the *Rocky Mount Evening Telegram*, Moore "got his shotgun and yelled to Collins to stop. The Negro turned, claimed Moore, "and as he turned, I shot." Collins, hit in the chest, ran off but was found later lying in a nearby yard. He was pronounced dead at a nearby hospital.

"He survived fighting in the Korean War only to be shot dead a few months after his honorable discharge while walking the streets of his hometown," Rick Collins would tell me of his father.

Newspaper clips from the time note that Moore was held on $1,000 bond while awaiting a probable cause hearing. But then, the clips stop. There is no coverage of a trial. No reporting on the response or reaction of the Collins family. Rick Collins told me that his father's killer was set free. The police, prosecutors, and judge took Moore's story at face value—that Collins had been acting suspiciously and that Moore was justified in shooting him—and simply let him go. "He never did a day of time for it," Rick told me of his father's killer. "He confessed that he did it, and yet he never served a day for doing it."

Now, decades later, he was determined that his son's killer would not have the same impunity.

According to the prosecutors, Urbanski had set off on a racist, homicidal path in 2016, when he began following a group on Facebook called Alt-Reich: Nation, one in a network of social media pages that sprouted up during the late Obama and early Trump years, communities where members of the self-proclaimed alt-right could share racist memes about Jews, immigrants, Muslims, and black people.

"His mind began to get poisoned with images of hate, racism, violence toward blacks, hatred of groups of people that don't look like him. His mind was being poisoned with these images that he was saving into his phone," prosecutor Jason Abbott told jurors in his opening statement. "On that night, all the students were drinking. Students were drinking up and down Route One at those bars. The defendant, though, when he was drinking, he was pouring gasoline onto a fire. This hatred that is in his mind is building up. Now he is drinking to the point where he is ready to act on that hatred."

For several minutes, prosecutors alleged, Urbanski had sat and watched his eventual victim. Done with the bars for the night, Collins and his friend Blake Bender had struck up a conversation with Amanda Lee, another college student waiting at the bus stop. They talked about their plans for after graduation. A couple of times, they all heard someone screaming in the woods up the street—"a nonsensical, angry scream," Bender would describe it—but they shrugged it off and kept talking. Neither of the men knew Lee, but Bender could tell that Collins thought she was cute and tried to play wingman. Before long, they all realized that the buses were no longer running and that they were all headed back to the University View apartment complex, so Lee began to call an Uber.

As they talked, Urbanski approached and unfolded his knife. He walked past Lee, an Asian woman, and Bender, a white man, and approached Collins. "Step left, step left if you know what's good for you," Urbanski demanded, his speech close to incoherent.

He repeated the command: "Step left if you know what's good for you."

"What?" Collins asked.

"Step left if you know what's good for you," Urbanski demanded a third time, to which Collins responded, "No."

Then, almost instantly, Urbanski thrust the blade into Collins's chest. Just as abruptly, Urbanski pulled the knife back out, folded it closed, clipped it to his front pants pocket, and fled.

"This poison that's spewing through his mind. . . . He was drinking to the point where now he lost his inhibition," the prosecutor insisted. "The courage that he didn't have to act on something while he was sober, now he has that courage. Beer muscles, liquid courage, that's what he had. With that hatred fueled in his mind, he is ready to act on it."

When it was the defense team's turn to address the court, Brennan argued that the prosecutor's case was based on speculation, not evidence. Not once, according to anyone there that night, had Urbanski uttered a racial slur. And prosecutors did not produce any witnesses to testify under oath that they'd ever heard him call for violence against black people. The racist memes on his phones were just a handful of images, out of more than seventeen thousand photos that he had saved. The prosecution's theory, and the Collins family's assertion, that their son had been targeted at all, much less due to his race, Brennan would argue, was "pure, unadulterated guesswork."

Yes, a black man was dead. Yes, the white man who killed him had been a member of a racist Facebook group and had racist cartoons saved on his phone. But could prosecutors *prove* that his intent and motivation had been racial animus? No, the defense insisted. Never mind that Urbanski's intent would have little pragmatic bearing on his crime's impact—that, to those victimized by racial prejudice, what matters is the real-world violence and the trauma that accompanies it, not a forensic autopsy of the perpetrator's motivations. Urbanski, the defense argued, had not set out to commit an act of hate. He was just belligerently drunk and inconsolably angry.

"The witnesses who were with Sean that evening will say that he was very drunk," Brennan explained. "They will also say he was angry. Was he angry at everyone? Was he angry at no one? Was he angry at himself? No one knows."

One theory, offered up by the defense, was that Urbanski was dreading the loneliness to come. He'd missed a semester of college, and so while the classmates he'd spent four years with were readying for the real world, he was being left behind. Leaving the bar that night, Urbanski had punched a street sign. Then, as his friends, the graduating seniors, went off to jump in the university fountain—a school tradition—he'd been left alone to brood. Richard Collins was the unfortunate victim of a random drunken act, of a crime "based on place, not race," the defense team insisted.

"They have talked about poison coursing through his veins. Huh? There is no manifesto. There is no speech. There will be no evidence that Sean ever marched, advocated, protested, did anything, anything of racial hatred. None whatsoever," Brennan told the jury.

"What there will be is evidence that Sean Urbanski was extraordinarily drunk that evening," he said, repeating the core of his defense. "The evidence will show that an extremely intoxicated young man who was angry at whom or what we don't know—classmates graduating, they are jumping in the fountain, and he's not—committed a drunken act that took the life of another human being. But that is not first-degree murder. It is not a hate crime."

Whether the killing of Richard Collins III amounted to murder would be for the jury to decide. But the ruling on whether prosecutors had met the hate crime standard would be decided by Judge Lawrence Hill.

There simply wasn't sufficient evidence that Collins had been killed *because* of his race, the defense argued, after requesting that the judge dismiss the hate crime charge. "The evidence indicates that our client approached three people . . . did not single out Richard Collins," a defense attorney argued. "There is no statement that was ever made related to race, or anything of that nature, from any of the witnesses who were present." As for the racist memes, the defense argued that there was no evidence that Urbanski had actually looked at any of the images that night.

In response, the prosecutors noted that of the three students at the bus stop, Collins, the black man, was the sole one to be stabbed. And they argued that the racist memes on Urbanski's phone couldn't be considered outside of the context of his membership in the Alt-Reich: Nation Facebook group. "That is no different than saying he was a member of the KKK," one of the prosecutors said in court. "The idea is it is an advocacy of violence and hatred and supremacy against those that are not like you."

This drew the ire of the defense team, which attempted to argue that it was "not true" to describe the Alt-Reich: Nation page—which has a name containing a direct reference to Nazi Germany—as equivalent to KKK membership and insisted instead that it was more accurately understood as "a joke site." Judge Hill, however, was sharp in his dismissal of this semantic pedantry. "But the memes are racist," he told the defense in rebuttal. "If this is a website or a group whose purpose is to . . . tell jokes, but the jokes are racist, then it's the same thing. It is still a white supremacist group. The ideology is the same. Because it is said in a laughing—or I will say a mocking—fashion doesn't make it any less racist."

While it was clear the prosecution had made its case for the murder charge, Judge Hill remained unconvinced about the hate crime charge. The statute, he noted, was worded very specifically. A person may not, "because of another person's race," commit or attempt to commit a crime against that person, "meaning that was the sole cause of what happened," the judge explained. There was no question, he went on, that Urbanski's racist views had been documented—he was a member of a white supremacist group on-line and had been so moved by several racist memes that he'd saved them to his phone's camera roll.

"The issue is," the judge continued, "did he strike him in the chest because he was black, or, I should say, did he strike him in the chest *only* because he was black?" That was the narrow legal question being considered that day, a stand-in for a broader societal question that cuts to the core of our understanding of racial bigotry and how it manifests in practice: When a racist kills a black person, is the murder itself necessarily racist?

No, the judge concluded, it is not. While a jury would still rule on the murder charges, Sean Urbanski would not be convicted of a hate crime for killing Richard Collins.

In January 2021, after years of delays, Sean Urbanski was sentenced to life in prison, with the possibility of parole after fifteen years. The judge agreed to have him sent to a special facility for youthful offenders.

But the Collins family continued fighting.

In October 2020, months before their son's killer would be sentenced, the Collinses succeeded in pushing for a change in an expansion of Maryland hate crime law; it will now apply to crimes committed "in whole or in part" by racial animus. Had that been the case during Urbanski's trial, it's likely he would have been found guilty of a hate crime. At least, Richard Collins's parents hope, the next family that experiences similar horror will have a chance at a level of justice that they were denied.

As the Trump years gave way to the Biden administration, much remained broken about the way the criminal legal system handles racial hatred. Groups, message boards, and online communities that traffic in bigotry remain commonplace. Law enforcement efforts to combat white radicalization and racial violence remain lackluster. And the burden of fighting for accountability still falls to the families of the victims.

It would be nice to be able to conclude that we've learned a lesson from this era of American Whitelash, but it's hard to look at the horizon and not see more horrors to come. The coarseness and demagoguing of the Trump era has not softened—and has, in fact, in many ways, intensified—in the years since he left office.

On the night of his election in 2008, Barack Obama had declared his ascent as proof that the dreams of the founders remained alive in our time. A decade and a half later, that dream has become a nightmare.

The same battles that accompanied the black presidency—debates about who belongs, what speech is acceptable in our public square, and who is responsible when bigotry's bark eventually turns into a devastating bite—remain at the fore of discourse. Black Americans, immigrants, and refugees continue to shape our culture, society, and democracy, demanding not just equality under law but also equity of outcome. In the meantime, the country's white majority grows increasingly agitated and aggrieved, convinced that it's all gone too far. All the while, an emboldened white supremacist movement stands eager to convert those disaffected citizens into soldiers for its cause.

Those white fears may be the defining force of our time, the undercurrent beneath the thrashing of our society, politics, and culture. And as long as there are elements within our mainstream politics and media willing to cynically play to those fears—unwilling to call racism and bigotry by their rightful names—we can expect additional bursts of white racial violence, the horrific calling card of our era of American Whitelash.

ACKNOWLEDGMENTS

This book would not have been possible without the participation of the families of many of those victimized by white supremacist violence, activists on the front lines of the battle for racial justice, and researchers who have made the study of hatred their life's work.

My agent Traci Wilkes Smith and my literary agent Anthony Mattero shepherded this, and all of my projects. Thanks to Alex Littlefield, for taking an underdeveloped idea and helping shape its scope and sweep, and to Rakia Clark, for believing in my vision and guiding it to the finish line. Philip Bashe's copyediting and fact-checking were essential. Any errors in this book are my own, despite his efforts.

As I first developed this book idea, Ibram Kendi made the crucial suggestion that I look at white supremacist attacks not just during the Trump years, but since Obama's election. Historian Taylor Branch helped me conceptualize the history of violent whitelash as less distinct time frames than a never-ending cycle. I benefited from early reads and feedback from Adam Serwer, Deanna Paul, and Daveen Trentman. Hannah Giorgis: you always remind me that everyone needs an editor; this book would have been impossible without you.

To my parents, brothers, and friends, including Melanie, Olivia, Freeman, Travis, the crew at Solly's, Dawsey, Toine, Jamerson, Lavanya, Tynes, Rem, Amanda and Joe, Vikkie, Ketchum, Skolnick, Karen, Chelsea, Gerrick, Errin, Colin, Gruber, Clint, Sean and Drew, and of course Priya (siren emoji) and Freddie.

NOTES

CHAPTER 1

5 *"Obama appealed to a belief in innocence":* Ta-Nehisi Coates, "My President Was Black," *The Atlantic* online, January/February 2017, https://www.theatlantic.com/magazine/archive/2017/01/my-president-was-black/508793.

7 *The white people acknowledged antiblack bias:* Michael I. Norton and Samuel R. Sommers, "Whites See Racism as a Zero-Sum Game That They Are Now Losing," *Perspectives on Psychological Science* 6, no. 3 (May 2011): 215–18.

7 *Two corresponding polls in 1986 and 2015:* Jim Tankersley and Scott Clement, "Young White People Are Losing Their Faith in the American Dream," *Washington Post*, December 1, 2015.

7 *By the end of the Obama presidency one year later: Discrimination in America: Experiences and Views of White Americans*, National Public Radio, Robert Wood Johnson Foundation, and Harvard T. H. Chan School of Public Health, November 2017, https://www.rwjf.org/en/library/research/2017/10/discrimination-in-america--experiences-and-views.html. Survey of 902 white U.S. adults conducted between January 26 and April 9, 2017.

8 *Frustrations with the limitations of a black president:* The phrase "black faces in high places" was popularized by Rashad Robinson, executive director of Color of Change, a civil rights group created during the

Bush-43 years—specifically, following Hurricane Katrina in 2005—
that would become one of the most influential in the country during
the Obama years.

9   *While the movement was concerned:* A March 2010 poll by researchers
    at the University of Washington found that only 35 percent of vot-
    ers who said they strongly approve of the Tea Party agreed with the
    statement that black Americans are hardworking (compared with 55
    percent of those who strongly disapproved of the Tea Party). Ac-
    cording to an April 2010 poll conducted by the *New York Times*, 52
    percent of self-described Tea Party voters said that in recent years
    "too much" had been made about the problems facing black Amer-
    icans, compared with 28 percent of all respondents. And in a poll
    released in November 2010 by the nonpartisan Public Religion Re-
    search Institute, 62 percent of white respondents who identified as
    Tea Party members believed that discrimination against whites had
    become as big a problem as discrimination against blacks and other
    minorities. (This compared with 56 percent of white Republicans,
    53 percent of white independents, and 30 percent of white Demo-
    crats.)

10 *"I was 17 when President-elect Obama":* Camonghne Felix, "The Fal-
    lacy of Representation," The Cut, last modified January 31, 2022,
    https://www.thecut.com/2022/01/fallacy-of-representation.html#_
    ga=2.251954958.62431037.1667004558-1802694257.1667004557.

12 *"Racial conservatives and those with the most punitive immigration
    views":* Tyler T. Reny, Loren Collingwood, and Ali A. Valenzuela,
    "Vote Switching in the 2016 Election: How Racial and Immigration
    Attitudes, Not Economics, Explain Shifts in White Voting," *Public
    Opinion Quarterly* 83, no. 1 (Spring 2019): 91–113.

13 *When a once-in-a-lifetime virus:* Daniel Wolfe and Daniel Dale, "'It's
    Going to Disappear': A Timeline of Trump's Claims That Covid-19
    Will Vanish," CNN online, last modified October 31, 2020, https://
    www.cnn.com/interactive/2020/10/politics/covid-disappearing
    -trump-comment-tracker/.

13 *Instead, Covid-19 drowned black, Latino, and indigenous communities:*
    Civil rights attorney and activist Sherrilyn Ifill, then head of the

NAACP Legal Defense Fund, described on Twitter the history that will one day be written about the coronavirus pandemic: "Many wondered, even in their final moments, how we came to be here. But the seeds had been planted and strewn and watered over decades of failures, of stubborn refusals to uproot the tares and bury the wages of the nation's original sin."

14 *"The people alleged by authorities"*: Robert A. Pape, "What an Analysis of 377 Americans Arrested or Charged in the Capitol Insurrection Tells Us," *Washington Post* online, April 6, 2021.

CHAPTER 2

15 *That same night, a pack of white teenagers:* Christine Hauser, "After a Hate Crime Spree, an Intense Effort to Make Arrests," *New York Times* online, January 11, 2009.

16 *The next morning, on the bus ride to school:* Jesse Washington, Associated Press, "Obama Election Spurs Race Crimes Around Country," *San Diego Union-Tribune* online, last modified November 16, 2008, https://www.sandiegouniontribune.com/sdut-obama-racial-111608 -2008nov16-story.html.

16 *Within just one week of Obama's election victory:* "Obama Win Sparks Rise in Hate Crimes, Violence," National Public Radio online, last modified November 25, 2008, https://www.npr.org/2008/11/25 /97454237/obama-win-sparks-rise-in-hate-crimes-violence.

16 *The first was an August 2008 report:* "Minorities Expected to Be Majority in 2050," CNN online, last modified August 13, 2008, https:// www.cnn.com/2008/US/08/13/census.minorities/.

17 *David Duke, for decades one of the nation's:* Southern Poverty Law Center online, "Hatemongers Poised to Exploit Obama Election, Tough Economic Times," news release, last modified January 29, 2009, https://www.splcenter.org/news/2009/01/21/hatemongers -poised-exploit-obama-election-tough-economic-times.

17 *Its adherents have long believed:* "We had badly underestimated the degree to which materialism had corrupted our fellow citizens, as well as the extent to which their feelings could be manipulated by

the mass media. As long as the government is able to keep the economy wheezing along, the people can be conditioned to accept any outrage."—Earl Turner, the fictional narrator of *The Turner Diaries*, a 1978 novel by white supremacist William Luther Pierce.

18 *Efforts to paint Obama as a foreign, Muslim invader:* In July 2009, after President Obama criticized a police officer in Cambridge, Massachusetts, for arresting Harvard University scholar Henry Louis Gates Jr. outside of his own home, Fox News host Glenn Beck declared, "This president, I think, has exposed himself as a guy, over and over and over again, who has a deep-seated hatred for white people or the white culture. I don't know what it is." He continued, "I'm not saying he doesn't like white people. I'm saying he has a problem. He has a—this guy is, I believe, a racist."

19 *"I can think of my godfather David Duke"*: Derek Black, interview by Michel Martin, *All Things Considered*, NPR, August 30, 2020, https:// www.keranews.org/2020-08-30/former-white-nationalist-on-rncs -racial-rhetoric.

20 *Federal hate crime data:* "President Trump's election was associated with a statistically significant surge in reported hate crimes across the United States, even when controlling for alternative explanations. Counties that voted for President Trump by the widest margins in the presidential election experienced the largest increases in reported hate crimes." Griffin Sims Edwards and Stephen Rushin, "The Effect of President Trump's Election on Hate Crimes" (working paper, SSRN, January 14, 2018), https://papers.ssrn.com/sol3 /papers.cfm?abstract_id=3102652.

"The FBI's annual reports on hate crime statistics show that hate crimes have increased from 6,121 incidents in 2016 to 7,314 in 2019, a 19.49 percent increase. Hate-motivated murders spiked to a total of 51 in 2019, the highest number in nearly 3 decades, according to an analysis of the FBI's data conducted by the Center for the Study of Hate and Extremism (CSHE) at California State University. . . . The CSHE found that 39 of the 51 hate-motivated murder victims in 2019 were killed by white supremacists, including the 23 victims killed in the August 3, 2019, mass shooting in El Paso, Texas." Daniel Villarreal, "Hate Crimes Under Trump Surged Nearly 20 Percent Says FBI Report," *Newsweek* online, last modified November 16, 2020, https://www.newsweek.com/hate-crimes-under-trump-surged -nearly-20-percent-says-fbi-report-1547870.

21   *In 2017 several colleagues and I at the* Washington Post *analyzed:* Wesley Lowery, Kimberly Kindy, and Andrew Ba Tran, "In the United States, Right-Wing Violence Is on the Rise," *Washington Post* online, November 25, 2018.

21   *Three years later, in September 2020:* Appearing before the House Homeland Security Committee on September 17, 2020, FBI director Christopher Wray testified: "What I can tell you is that, within the domestic terrorism bucket category as a whole, racially motivated violent extremism is, I think, the biggest bucket within that larger group, and within the racially motivated violent extremists bucket, people subscribing to some kind of white supremacist–type ideology is certainly the biggest chunk of that." He added later: "Racially motivated violent extremists over recent years have been responsible for the most lethal activity in the U.S."

CHAPTER 3

25   *I was less interested in the debate:* And to be clear, racial prejudice was among several prominent themes that helped build Trump's coalition.

25   *"Think I stab motherfuckers in the neck for fun?":* Multnomah County Circuit Court affidavit, filed May 30, 2017.

CHAPTER 4

33   *While immigrants accounted for just 4.8 percent:* Abby Budiman, "Key Findings About U.S. Immigrants," Pew Research Center online, last modified August 20, 2020, https://www.pewresearch.org/fact -tank/2020/08/20/key-findings-about-u-s-immigrants/.

33   *That number would soar to nineteen million:* Marta Tienda and Susana

Sanchez, "Latin American Immigration to the United States," *Daedalus* 142, no. 3 (Summer 2013): 48–64, doi:10.1162/DAED_a_00218.

33 *"Everyone seemed to be migrating north"*: Mirta Ojito, *Hunting Season: Immigration and Murder in an All-American Town* (Boston: Beacon Press, 2013), 38.

35 *"We had to show our power"*: Saul Gonzalez, "Hundreds of Thousands Marched for Immigrant Rights a Decade Ago. What's Happened Since?," *The World* online, last modified March 30, 2016, https://theworld.org/stories/2016-03-30/hundreds-thousands-marched-immigrant-rights-decade-ago-whats-happened.

35 *"They are worried about a system"*: Comprehensive Immigration Reform Act of 2006, Congressional Record 152, no. 67, S9562 (May 25, 2006).

36 *earned Senate passage but ultimately failed:* The Senate would again pass sweeping immigration reform in 2013, only for Republican leaders in the House to deny it a vote.

36 *In 2006 the* New York Times: David Leonhardt, "Immigrants and Prison," *New York Times* online, May 30, 2007.

36 *In the years to come:* A *Time* magazine poll at the time showed that 72 percent of Americans approved of a guest worker program. Mark Schulman and Tara Regan, "Poll Analysis: Large Majority Favors 'Guest Workers,'" *Time* online, March 31, 2006.

37 *Dobbs's six o'clock evening news hour:* Dobbs did not reply to my attempts to reach him for an interview.

37 *Limbaugh proclaimed in a 2007 radio segment:* Rush Limbaugh, "Immigration Bill Must Be Defeated," *The Rush Limbaugh Show*, aired May 21, 2007, transcript available at https://www.rushlimbaugh.com/daily/2007/05/21/immigration_bill_must_be_defeated/.

38 *His campaign would go on to describe her:* Eric Zorn, "In Roskam's Hands, Truth Gets Slippery," *Chicago Tribune* online, September 21, 2006.

38 *Ultimately, Roskam won the election by 4,810 votes:* Duckworth would go on to win a different congressional seat in 2012 and be elected to the Senate in 2016. Roskam served twelve years in Congress and ascended to the Republican House leadership before being defeated by a Democratic challenger in 2018.

39 *And the Great Recession, as it came to be known:* David Goldman, "Work Harder, Take Home Less," CNN Money online, last modified August 28, 2008, https://money.cnn.com/2008/08/27/news/economy /state_of_working_america/index.htm.

CHAPTER 5

42 *Beginning in the 1920s:* "Selected U.S. Immigration Legislation and Executive Actions, 1790–2014," Pew Research Center online, last modified September 28, 2015, https://www.pewresearch.org /hispanic/2015/09/28/selected-u-s-immigration-legislation-and -executive-actions-1790-2014/.

43 *By the time of the Rock Springs Massacre in 1885:* Jeff Wallenfeldt, "There's a Riot Goin' On: Riots in U.S. History (Part One)," *Encyclopædia Britannica* online, accessed January 2021. https://www .britannica.com/list/10-fascinating-facts-about-the-first-americans.

43 *Chinese workers were farming in countless American fields:* Tom Rea, "The Rock Springs Massacre," Wyoming State Historical Society online, last modified November 8, 2014, https://www.wyohistory .org/encyclopedia/rock-springs-massacre.

44 *By 1885, there were six hundred Chinese miners:* Rea, "Rock Springs Massacre."

44 *Throughout that summer, there had been reports:* Rea, "Rock Springs Massacre."

44 *"It is said that the mine bosses have favored":* "The Massacre of the Chinese," *New-York Times*, September 5, 1885, 5.

45 *When Governor Francis E. Warren traveled to Rock Springs:* "Massacre of the Chinese," 5.

45 *As the historian John V. Baiamonte Jr. notes:* John V. Baiamonte Jr., "'Who Killa de Chief' Revisited: The Hennessey Assassination and Its Aftermath, 1890–1991," *Louisiana History: The Journal of the Louisiana Historical Association* 33, no. 2 (Spring 1992): 117–46, https:// www.jstor.org/stable/4232935.

46 *Brent Staples of the* New York Times *writes:* Brent Staples, "How Italians Became 'White,'" Opinion, *New York Times* online, October 12,

2019,   https://www.nytimes.com/interactive/2019/10/12/opinion
/columbus-day-italian-american-racism.html?searchResultPosition=1.

46   *"It shouldn't matter if a group of people"*: Joe Ragazzo, "On Indigenous
Peoples' Day and the Cleveland Guardians," Rapsody, last modified
October 12, 2021, https://ragazzo.substack.com/p/on-indigenous
-peoples-day-and-the.

47   *"When the first Africans arrived in Virginia"*: Theodore W. Allen, *The
Invention of the White Race*, vol. 1, *Racial Oppression and Social Control*
(New York: Verso, 1994).

48   *"Race supplied the key to resolving these conflicts"*: James D. Rice, *Tales
from a Revolution: Bacon's Rebellion and the Transformation of Early
America* (New York: Oxford University Press, 2012).

52   *The editorial board of the* New-York Times *disparaged:* "The New-
Orleans Affair," *New-York Times*, March 16, 1891, 4.

52   *The headline:* "No Mercy Was Shown," *Washington Post*, March 15,
1891, 1.

52   *"Monday we dined at the Camerons; various dago diplomats were present"*: Theodore Roosevelt to Anna Roosevelt, March 21, 1891,
Theodore Roosevelt Collection. MS Am 1834 (307), Harvard College Library, https://www.theodorerooseveltcenter.org/Research
/Digital-Library/Record?libD=o2980928; Theodore Roosevelt Digital Library, Dickinson State University.

53   *The U.S. government agreed to pay reparations:* "A Settlement with It-
aly," *New-York Times*, April 15, 1892, 4.

53   *In April 2019, nearly 130 years later:* Chris Finch, "Mayor LaToya
Cantrell Issues Proclamation of Apology for Italian Lynching in
1891," FOX 8 online, last modified April 12, 2019, https://www.fox-
8live.com/2019/04/12/mayor-latoya-cantrell-issue-apology-italian-
lynching/.

53   *Hundreds of white men stalked the streets:* Johanna Miller, "Watsonville
Apologizes to Filipino Community for 1930 Race Riots," *Good Times*
online (Santa Cruz, CA), last modified November 13, 2020, https://
www.goodtimes.sc/watsonville-apologizes-to-filipino-community
-for-1930-race-riots/.

54 *A twenty-two-year-old man named Fermin Tobera:* Tony Nunez, "It's Time to Honor Fermin Tobera," *Pajaronian* (Watsonville, CA) online, last modified January 31, 2020, https://pajaronian.com/its-time -to-honor-fermin-tobera-tonys-thoughts/.

54 *"We like Mexicans, and we think they like us":* "Editorial: An Examination of *The Times'* Failures on Race, Our Apology and a Path Forward," Opinion, *Los Angeles Times* online, last modified September 27, 2020, https://www.latimes.com/opinion/story/2020-09-27 /los-angeles-times-apology-racism.

54 *"It had to come":* Colin Campbell, "Two Nights of Rioting Bring a Curfew to Lawrence, Mass," *New York Times*, August 11, 1984, 1.

54 *Four years later, in 1988:* John Killen, "Portland's Past: Skinhead Murder of Mulugeta Seraw on Nov. 13, 1988, Shook the City," *Oregonian* (Portland, OR) online, last modified November 13, 2014, https://www.oregonlive.com/history/2014/11/portlands_past_skin head_murder.html.

55 *"Almost overnight, the South Side emerged":* Adam Green, "How a Brutal Race Riot Shaped Modern Chicago," Opinion, *New York Times* online, August 3, 2019, https://www.nytimes.com/2019/08/03 /opinion/how-a-brutal-race-riot-shaped-modern-chicago.html? searchResultPosition=1.

56 *The violence continued for thirteen days:* The Red Summer of 1919, The Chicago History Museum, Julius L. Jones.

56 *resulting in thirty-eight deaths . . . thousand homeless families:* Abigail Higgins, "Red Summer of 1919: How Black WWI Vets Fought Back Against Racist Mobs," History.com, last modified December 2, 2009, https://www.history.com/news/red-summer-1919-riots-chicago-dc -great-migration.

56 *The Negro in Chicago:* Chicago Commission on Race Relations, *The Negro in Chicago: A Study of Race Relations and a Race Riot* (Chicago: University of Chicago Press, 1922).

56 *Upon their arrival:* Martin Luther King Jr., "Chicago Campaign," in *The Autobiography of Martin Luther King, Jr.*, ed. Clayborne Carson (New York: Warner Books, 1998).

56   *"I have seen many demonstrations"*: "Dr. King Is Felled by Rock," *Chicago Tribune*, August 6, 1966, 1.

CHAPTER 7

71   *"Phantom-like hosts"*: Terence McArdle, "The Day 30,000 White Supremacists in KKK Robes Marched in the Nation's Capital," *Washington Post*, August 11, 2018, https://www.washingtonpost.com/news/retropolis/wp/2017/08/17/the-day-30000-white-supremacists-in-kkk-robes-marched-in-the-nations-capital/.

72   *"Congress was deluged with letters"*: David R. Roediger, *Working Toward Whiteness: How America's Immigrants Became White* (New York: Basic Books, 2005).

CHAPTER 8

76   *Friends of the family*: Anne Barnard, "Admired by Many, but to Police a Killer," *New York Times*, November 24, 2008, 25.

77   *"He comes from a family"*: William Keahon did not respond to my requests to reach him for comment.

78   *"I'm nothing like what the papers said about me"*: Bob Conroy died in 2015. The Conroy family did not respond to my request for an interview. Jeff Conroy did not respond to letters sent to him in prison.

78   *"I'm not a white supremacist or anything like that"*: Manny Fernandez, "In Jail, Hate Crime Killer Says He Isn't So Hateful," *New York Times*, April 29, 2010, 19.

CHAPTER 9

85   *Two days after Trump's 2016 presidential victory*: Mike Levine, "'No Blame?' ABC News Finds 54 Cases Invoking 'Trump' in Connection with Violence, Threats, Alleged Assaults," ABC News online, last modified May 30, 2020, https://abcnews.go.com/Politics/blame-abc-news-finds-17-cases-invoking-trump/story?id=58912889.

86   *"The people who carry out these attacks are already violent"*: Peter Baker
     and Michael D. Shear, "In Texas Gunman's Manifesto, an Echo of
     Trump's Language," *New York Times*, August 4, 2019, 1.

CHAPTER 10

91   *The forty-year-old skinhead had moved*: My account of Wade Michael
     Page's life in Milwaukee prior to the shooting is based largely on FBI
     investigative files that have since been made public.

91   *white supremacist message boards*: John Diedrich, "FBI Warrant Details
     Sikh Temple Shooter's Online White Power Searches," *Milwaukee
     Journal-Sentinel* online, May 13, 2013, https://archive.jsonline.com
     /news/milwaukee/fbi-warrant-details-sikh-temple-shooters-online
     -white-power-searches-jr9uddl-207291121.html/.

CHAPTER 11

95   *And, in the weeks before my visit to Iowa*: "Brussels Attacks: First Anni-
     versary of Bombings Marked," BBC online, last modified March 22,
     2017, https://www.bbc.com/news/world-europe-39350005.

95   *Ted Cruz . . . called for police agencies to "patrol and secure Muslim com-
     munities before they become radicalized"*: Katie Zezima and Adam Gold-
     man, "Ted Cruz Calls for Law Enforcement to 'Patrol and Secure'
     Muslim Neighborhoods," *Washington Post* online, March 22, 2016.

96   *In 2008 three Tennessee men spray-painted swastikas*: "Combatting
     Post-9/11 Discriminatory Backlash," U.S. Department of Justice
     online, last modified August 6, 2015, https://www.justice.gov/crt
     /combating-post-911-discriminatory-backlash-6.

96   *Each year for the next decade*: Brian Levin, "Explaining the Rise in
     Hate Crimes Against Muslims in the U.S.," *Elko (NV) Daily Free Press*
     online, last modified April 11, 2019, https://elkodaily.com/opinion
     /columnists/explaining-the-rise-in-hate-crimes-against-muslims
     -in-the-us/article_f392b1c9-d1e5-5fc3-9ded-c6ce7d4465e0.html.

96   *Balbir Singh Sodhi was planting flowers*: Valarie Kaur, "His Brother

Was Murdered for Wearing a Turban After 9/11. 15 Years Later, He Spoke to the Killer," *The World* online, last modified September 23, 2016, https://theworld.org/stories/2016-09-23/his-brother -was-murdered-wearing-turban-after-911-last-week-he-spoke-killer.

CHAPTER 13

110   *"I could see from the back seat"*: "A Mother Tries to Atone for a Deadly Hate Crime," *Morning Edition*, NPR online, last modified August 17, 2012, https://www.npr.org/2012/08/17/158926181/a-murder -a-secret-and-a-mothers-attempt-to-atone.

113   *"I realized in that moment"*: "How a Gang of Skinheads Forever Changed the Course of *The Oprah Winfrey Show*," *The Oprah Winfrey Show*, aired on May 13, 2011, available on *The Oprah Winfrey Show* online, https://www.oprah.com/own-oprahshow/how-a-gang-of-skin -heads-changed-oprah-show-history-video.

CHAPTER 14

121   *kill Michigan governor Gretchen Whitmer*: Margaret Huang, "Oklahoma City Bombing: 26 Years Later, the Same Extremist Threats Prevail," SPLC online, April 22, 2021, https://www.splcenter.org /news/2021/04/22/oklahoma-city-bombing-26-years-later-same -extremist-threats-prevail.

122   *Five militia leaders were brought before the committee:* Lori Montgomery, Knight-Ridder, "Militia Witnesses Try to Convince Senators— Testimony Ranges from Bizarre to Scary at Senate Hearings," *Spokesman-Review* (Spokane, WA), June 16, 1995, 1.

127   *A U.S. Justice Department audit would later find:* Vera Bergengruen and W. J. Hennigan, "'We Are Being Eaten from Within.' Why America Is Losing the Battle Against White Nationalist Terrorism," *Time* online, last modified August 8, 2019, https://time.com/5647304/white -nationalist-terrorism-united-states/.

131   *"I think it is important for all of us to remember"*: When I reached Rehbein in March 2020, he declined to discuss Johnson's report and the contro-

versy that ensued. "With that being eleven years ago, I am not sure that I would completely trust the accuracy of my memory," he said. "I think it would be best if we simply let the published record speak for itself."

CHAPTER 15

133 *"The way for local police to secure their communities"*: Michael German, "Soon, We'll All Be Radicals," ACLU online, last modified April 16, 2009, https://www.aclu.org/news/national-security/soon-well-all-be-radicals.

134 *"This report appears to have blurred the line"*: Representative Bennie Thompson (D-MS), chairman, U.S. House Committee on Homeland Security, to Janet Napolitano, secretary, U.S. Department of Homeland Security, April 14, 2009, available at Federation of American Scientists (FAS) online, https://fas.org/irp/congress/2009_cr/hsc041409.pdf.

135 *In 2011 the* Washington Post *reported:* R. Jeffrey Smith, "Homeland Security Department Curtails Home-grown Terror Analysis," *Washington Post* online, June 7, 2011.

CHAPTER 18

148 *Frazier Glenn Miller Jr. had been barking:* Holly Henry, "Suspect in Jewish Center Shootings 'Entrenched in the Hate Movement,'" WTKR (Hampton, VA) online, last modified April 14, 2014, https://www.wtkr.com/2014/04/14/suspect-in-jewish-center-shootings-entrenched-in-the-hate-movement.

149 *in his self-published autobiography:* Glenn Miller, *A White Man Speaks Out*, self-published, October 4, 1999.

CHAPTER 19

155 *"Because of what I did, Jews feel less secure"*: Judy L. Thomas, "F. Glenn Miller Jr. Talks for the First Time About Killings at Jewish Centers," *Kansas City Star* online, November 15, 2014.

CHAPTER 20

163 *In the years to come, she'd drift deeper and deeper:* D. J. Cashmere, "Deradicalization in the Deep South: How a Former Neo-Nazi Makes Amends," *YES!* online, last modified November 12, 2019, https://www.yesmagazine.org/issue/building-bridges/2019/11/12 /deradicalization-in-the-deep-south.

163 *"I only hung out with other white supremacists":* Toby Tabachnick, "She Was 'a Neo-Nazi Skinhead,'" *Pittsburgh Jewish Chronicle* online, last modified November 14, 2019, https://jewishchronicle.timesofisrael .com/she-was-a-neo-nazi-skinhead/.

CHAPTER 21

170 *Oscar himself had been arrested five times:* Demian Bulwa, "Oscar Grant's Character, Shooter Both on Trial," *San Francisco Chronicle* online, last modified May 30, 2010, https://www.sfgate.com/crime /article/Oscar-Grant-s-character-shooter-both-on-trial-3186791 .php.

CHAPTER 22

174 *"We were the same age":* Huda Mu'min, "Ryan Coogler on 'Fruitvale Station,'" *Washington Post* online, July 21, 2013.

CHAPTER 25

189 *"The only reason the narrative about conditions":* Clark Randall and Jamiles Lartey, "'A Hopeless Place': St. Louis Workhouse Denounced as a Modern-Day Debtors' Prison," *Guardian* (U.S. edition) online, last modified September 24, 2018, https://www.theguardian .com/us-news/2018/sep/24/i-feel-like-a-slave-st-louis-workhouse -denounced-as-a-modern-day-debtors-prison.

CHAPTER 28

198   *When Clark stepped in to pull his girlfriend away:* Tim Nelson, "Con-
      flicting Accounts: What Happened the Night Jamar Clark Was
      Shot?," Minnesota Public Radio online, last modified Decem-
      ber 4, 2015, https://www.mprnews.org/story/2015/12/04/jamarclark
      -shooting-what-happened.

201   *They also found photos of him:* News release, Hennepin County attor-
      ney's office, 2015, https://www.hennepinattorney.org/-/media/cao
      /news/2015/scarsella-11-30-15.pdf.

201   *Just hours before the shooting:* John Croman, "Trial Exhibits Reveal
      Scarsella's Racist Rhetoric," KARE 11 (Minnesota) online, last mod-
      ified February 12, 2017, https://www.kare11.com/article/news/trial
      -exhibits-reveal-scarsellas-racist-rhetoric/406976678.

202   *Ultimately, he was given fifteen years in prison:* "Man Gets 15 Years
      for Shooting 5 Black Lives Matter Protesters," CBS News (Min-
      nesota) online, last modified April 26, 2017, https://www.cbsnews
      .com/news/minnesota-man-gets-15-years-for-shooting-5-black
      -lives-matter-protesters/.

CHAPTER 29

206   *And in 1902 the state legislature approved:* Brent Tarter, "African Amer-
      icans and Politics in Virginia (1865–1902)," Encyclopedia Virginia,
      last modified December 14, 2020, https://encyclopediavirginia.org
      /entries/african-americans-and-politics-in-virginia-1865-1902.

CHAPTER 30

211   *"These folks couldn't run a two-car parade":* Sandy Hausman, "Mayor
      Calls Charlottesville 'Capital of Resistance,'" Radio IQ WVTF (Vir-
      ginia) online, last modified January 31, 2017, https://www.wvtf.org
      /news/2017-01-31/mayor-calls-charlottesville-capital-of-resistance.

212 *"I think one thing that I have in common"*: Ian Shapira, "Inside Jason Kessler's Hate-Fueled Rise," *Washington Post* online, August 11,
2018.

CHAPTER 31

218 *It was unclear that he was a member:* James Pilcher, "Charlottesville
Suspect's Beliefs Were 'Along the Party Lines of the Neo-Nazi
Movement,' Ex-Teacher Says," *Cincinnati Enquirer* online, last
modified August 13, 2017, https://www.cincinnati.com/story/news
/local/northern-ky/2017/08/13/charlottesville-suspects-beliefs-were
-along-party-lines-neo-nazi-movement-ex-teacher-says/563139001/.

218 *cruel policies:* Allison Reamer and Lauren Lindstrom, "Teacher Says
Suspected Charlottesville Driver James Alex Fields Jr. Showed Extremist Ideologies in High School," Block News Alliance, August 13,
2017, accessed online via the *Pittsburgh Post-Gazette*, https://www
.post-gazette.com/news/nation/2017/08/13/James-Alex-Fields
-Charlottesville-killing-driver-car-crowd-white-nationalist-rally
/stories/201708130175.

222 *"To offer an accurate diagnosis"*: "Statement of Ms. Susan Bro, Co-
founder, President, and Board Chair, Heather Heyer Foundation,
House Committee on Oversight and Reform Subcommittee on
Civil Rights and Civil Liberties, 'Confronting White Supremacy
(Part I): The Consequences of Inaction,'" Wednesday, May 15,
2019, available at Heather Heyer Foundation online, https://www
.congress.gov/116/meeting/house/109478/witnesses/HHRG-116
-GO02-Wstate-BroS-20190515-U2.pdf.

Barbara Sprunt, "Here's What the New Hate Crimes Law Aims to
Do As Attacks on Asian Americans Rise," NPR online, last modified
May 20, 2021, https://www.npr.org/2021/05/20/998599775/biden
-to-sign-the-covid-19-hate-crimes-bill-as-anti-asian-american-attacks
-rise.